ENDORSEMENTS

The Science of Deliverance is a must-have tool for our equipping network deliverance ministers. It is a recommended resource of maintenance for all those to whom we minister healing and deliverance! This book will open your eyes to see the depth of the beauty in God's creation of man through the microscope of modern science empowering people to minister to others in healing prayer more effectively. Jareb and Petra Nott take what could be a heady subject and make it easy for the average layman. I highly recommend this book!

APRIL FARRIS
Apostolic leader, LivingStones
Communities Equipping Network
Cleveland, Ohio

I am so excited that Jareb and Petra have written a book about the deliverance and cleansing of the DNA. From the time of Genesis 3:15 until now, satan has been working to corrupt the DNA of mankind to stop the purposes of God for each person and the earth.

Friedrich Miescher discovered DNA in the late 1860s even though DNA was created in the beginning with the creation of Adam. Many of the secrets of understanding DNA were not unveiled till the 1950s by James Watson and Francis Crick when they became the first scientists to formulate an accurate description of the DNA molecule's complex, double-helical structure.

DNA is our own personal instruction book planted in us by the Creator. That is why satan and his forces pursue the control of DNA so relentlessly. This book is on time for us now to bring our DNA back to its original intent. Now is the time that our instruction book was back in the hands of the Creator of all, Yahweh.

Life provides an awesome testimony to the creative genius of God. King David expressed God's creation of every detail of man so well by writing: *"For You formed my inward parts; You covered me in my mother's womb. I will praise You, for I am fearfully and wonderfully made; marvelous are Your works, and that my soul knows very well"* (Ps. 139:13-14).

Jareb and Petra are doing remarkable work in the deliverance ministry and now are sharing their understanding of how to bring DNA back into correct alignment. This book is for everyone and is an invaluable asset to a deliverance minister. I would suggest this work becomes a guide in the deliverance ministry and in training deliverance ministers.

RUTH ANN MCDONALD
Global Vision Faith Center
Philadelphia, MS

Finally, a book that explores what we knew all along—the idea that science and the medical field are confirming the power of our words, thought life, and the ability to change from the inside out. Jareb and Petra Nott have written a must-read, easy-to-understand guide to understanding the transformation of the physical body in response to spiritual realities with the help of scientific evidence.

REV. MARY ANN YOUNG
VP of Operations, Cleansing Stream International

In their book, *The Science of Deliverance*, Jareb and Petra Nott give us a practical yet powerful prescription for living in freedom and wholeness, body, soul, and spirit. Their approach is both biblical and balanced and demonstrates the bridge between the spirit realm and science as well as the connection between healing and deliverance. This book will empower the reader to employ prayers, proclamations, and principles that will result in the manifestation of supernatural miracles in every area of life. Thank you, Jareb and Petra, for this masterful work that will release life and victory to many.

JANE HAMON
Apostle, Vision Church @ Christian International
Author of *Dreams and Visions, The Cyrus Decree, The Deborah Company, Discernment and Declarations for Breakthrough*, and more

the SCIENCE of DELIVERANCE

How Spiritual Freedom Brings Physical Healing

JAREB & PETRA NOTT

DESTINY IMAGE® PUBLISHERS, INC.

P.O. Box 310, Shippensburg, PA 17257-0310

"Promoting Inspired Lives."

This book and all other Destiny Image and Destiny Image Fiction books are available at Christian bookstores and distributors worldwide.

Cover design by Eileen Rockwell

Interior design by Terry Clifton

For more information on foreign distributors, call 717-532-3040.

Reach us on the Internet: www.destinyimage.com.

ISBN 13 TP: 978-0-7684-6199-2

ISBN 13 eBook: 978-0-7684-6200-5

For Worldwide Distribution, Printed in the U.S.A.

1 2 3 4 5 6 7 8 / 25 24 23 22 21

DEDICATION

To Greg and Becca Greenwood, who continually challenge us to move into the next step God has for us, and then mentor us through it so that we don't kill ourselves in the process. They were catalysts in getting this adventure started, and we count their guidance and friendship as one of our greatest blessings!

CONTENTS

FOREWORD

John 8:32 teaches us, *"You will know the truth, and the truth will set you free."* Our heavenly Father desires that each of His children walk in victory and freedom in every area of their lives. It is not just truth that sets us free but *knowing* the truth that sets us free. When we as children of God know the truth and understand that we are to be delivered from unhealthy emotions and wrong thinking and live victorious over demonic strongholds and walk in supernatural healing and wholeness, we are empowered to partner with the Lord to claim our victory. We can then become independent from the lies of darkness, demonic strongholds, our wounded emotions, and the resulting infirmities. We can learn to control our thoughts and to think on good things, on the goodness of God, and on His Word. We can praise and exalt the Lord and, as a result, disarm the enemy and find life-changing freedom. Allow me to share a powerful testimony to this truth.

It was a particularly warm evening in Africa with no air conditioning in the building. I have to confess, I was not feeling favorable toward engaging in a long altar-ministry time due to the heat that night. However, as I spoke, the Lord clearly directed me to teach on the lies of a stronghold of rejection and the power of forgiveness to see this stronghold defeated. The Spirit of God moved mightily on people's hearts, as many wept throughout the message.

Upon completing the teaching, I invited everyone who wanted freedom to make their way to the altar. As people were walking to the front, the Lord highlighted one young woman to me. She wore a hat pulled down over her forehead in an obvious attempt to avoid having to make eye contact with others. She continually looked down to the ground and was extremely soft-spoken. I laid hands on her and began to pray.

The Lord showed me that this woman had been abused repeatedly as a child. I gently asked her, "What is your name?" and in a whisper she responded, "Miriam." I then shared with her what the Lord showed me: "Miriam, I feel the Lord is showing me that as a little girl you were repeatedly abused. Is this true?" Shyly she nodded her head in agreement. Based on the message I had shared that night, she understood that unforgiveness would keep her bound by traumas from the past and block her emotional healing. Of course, I explained to her that forgiveness and trust are not the same thing—the Lord would not want her to entrust herself to someone who continually abused her or to put herself back in harm's way. But it was necessary for her to forgive so that she would no longer be bound by rejection, fear, depression, torment in her mind and emotions, and oppression in her physical body.

Miriam willingly forgave the man who had brought such hurt and pain into her life. As she did, I prayed that the lies of these strongholds in her mind and emotions would be broken and that the love of the Lord would bring healing to her. She began to weep tears of joy as the Lord touched her powerfully.

I hugged Miriam and then made a request of her: "Miriam, you do not need to cover your beauty with this hat. You are a beautiful woman, and the Lord wants you to have good and healthy relationships. I don't want you to walk with your eyes always shamefully cast to the ground. You need to take this hat off and walk with your head held up and a smile on your face, rejoicing in the Lord and His love. You are a beautiful daughter of the King of kings, and He desires that you experience the fullness of His love, joy, peace, and acceptance. I would like to request that tomorrow when you attend this conference, you come to me without this hat on, and give me a big hug and a report on your spiritual condition." She smiled and agreed to do as I suggested.

The following morning, our ministry team was waiting for the elevator to go to the sanctuary for the first morning session. A strikingly beautiful young woman approached and stood waiting at the elevator beside us. She smiled at me, and I graciously smiled back. Then she spoke to me in a questioning voice: "You do not recognize me?" Trying to place her in my mind, I asked, "Have we met before?" She said gently, "I am Miriam." Thinking that I had misheard the name, I asked, "What is your name again?" She smiled a confident smile and said, "I am Miriam, the girl with the hat! You prayed for me last night. I am free!"

Friends, I was elated and startled all at the same time. I had never witnessed such a dramatic change so quickly in someone to whom I had ministered. This woman did not look at all like the same person. Everyone waiting for the elevator broke out in joyous laughter and weeping. I embraced Miriam and wept tears of joy with her. God had so miraculously set her free that within this twelve-hour period of time she was a completely transformed young woman. Forgiving her perpetrator had transformed Miriam's life immediately.

The apostle Paul offers this insight: *"May God himself, the God of peace, sanctify you through and through. May your whole spirit, soul and body be kept blameless at the coming of our Lord Jesus Christ"* (1 Thess. 5:23).

The spirit, soul, and body make up the whole or entire man. The Greek word for *complete* is *holothesis*. It is defined as "complete to the end, perfect, undamaged, whole through and through." To be found blameless at Jesus' coming, therefore, we must allow the Lord to work completely or through and through our entire being, which comprises these three separate entities.

We are spirit, soul, and body. God designed us so that the soul and body would be led by the spirit part of ourselves—the part that the enemy could not touch. Through Adam's disobedience, however, man entered spiritual death. Now Adam and his children would find that the willful soul would seek dominance in determining their thoughts and actions.

The good news is Jesus restored our broken relationship with the Father. Thus, when we are born again, things change. Our spirits are revived from death to life and can again enjoy intimate communion with the Lord. And because evil cannot reside in the presence of the Lord, our spirits are safe from the enemy's grasp. Our souls, however, are a different story. They remain open to the devil's attack—just as Adam's mind, not his spirit, was open to deception before the fall. It is in our souls—our minds, wills, and emotions—that the spirits of darkness harass, oppress, and influence us.

Demons and demonic strongholds not only attach themselves to our souls but also use our bodies to operate through to fulfill their evil desire, and many times the result is to also inflict harm and sickness in our personal lives and down our family lines. Demons embrace the personality of their namesake. A spirit of perversion, for example, is perverse. This particular lustful demon needs a body to function through in order to fulfill its lustful desires. Another example is a spirit of bondage. This demon is responsible for all kinds of addictions. Whenever alcoholism, food disorders, pornography, and drugs become addictive, a spirit of bondage has established a stronghold. It is through the individual that the demons experience the drugs, alcohol, pornography, and any other addictions it longs for. Just as unhealthy choices and lifestyles affect and bring harm to our physical bodies, likewise unholy and sinful choices affect our mind, will, emotions, and physical bodies. Born-again Christians, therefore, can embrace sinful thoughts and practices and also be held captive to a foothold of generational strongholds that unlock a door for the demonic.

What is a generational iniquity or stronghold? Exodus 20:4-6 explains:

> *No carved gods of any size, shape, or form of anything whatever, whether of things that fly or walk or swim. Don't bow down to them and don't serve them because I am God, your God, and I'm a most jealous God,*

punishing the children for any sins their parents pass on to them to the third, and yes, even to the fourth generation of those who hate me. But I'm unswervingly loyal to the thousands who love me and keep my commandments (MSG).

The actual Hebrew word used in this scripture for *sin* is *avown*. It is translated "iniquity, guilt, a judicial state of being liable for a wrong done." If past generations have worshiped idols, turned their backs on God, and/or hated Him, it is an open door for strongholds to be passed down the family line. The good news is Jesus brought forgiveness, grace, and mercy: *"His mercy extends to those who fear him, from generation to generation"* (Luke 1:50). Therefore, we can repent on behalf of the sin in our family line, be set free from its demonic grip, and provide a righteous inheritance for ourselves and the generations to come.

This leads us to the truths that Jareb and Petra Nott explain vividly in the scribed message of this manuscript. How science is confirming what the Word of God has always taught us. That sin, generational iniquity, wrong thinking, emotional trauma, fear, anxiety, rejection, and unforgiveness does indeed negatively affect our entire being, which includes our physical bodies. The truth is our spirit, soul, and body are to be found blameless at the coming of the Lord. And the truth is He wants us free!

This manuscript is brilliantly written and packed full of powerful insight of how science, though the study of epigenetics, proves that we can be impacted by sin, trauma, wrong thinking patterns, and generational iniquity. But the more poignant truth is how radically our DNA is transformed from dark to light when the delivering truth, power, glory, and love of the Lord is welcomed and received in our lives.

Acts 2:2 shares a transformational promise, when the Holy Spirit *"filled the whole house where they were sitting."* The "whole house" meant the room, each person in that room, a temple or meeting place of the Lord, the entire family line from generation to generation, and the property and possessions associated with a house or household (Strong's #G3624). Meaning that the family line is now marked to have the choice to receive this awesome, glorious gift and all the inherited kingdom promises made known through Holy Spirit! What an awesome prayer strategy when praying for our family, our homes, and our possessions—praying from the promise of the blessing that is placed on our personal lives and our family line when we are filled with the Spirit of God. What the enemy means for harm in our lives and our family bloodlines, Holy Spirit presence and fire marks us with the promise of power, victory, and freedom. Through the name of Jesus, the blood of Jesus, the love of Jesus, and Holy Spirit empowerment, we have the promise and kingdom inheritance to be transformed spirit, soul, and body, even at the molecular and DNA level of our beings.

Friends, this book will empower you into transformational action to grab hold of and walk in victorious freedom and healing. By identifying strongholds operating in our personal lives or operating down the family bloodline, you will be empowered to overcome, conquer, and demolish the schemes of the enemy and to walk the abundant life promised and made available to us through our heavenly Father, Jesus, and Holy Spirit. Thank you, Jareb and Petra, for such a timely now word and message.

Rebecca Greenwood
Cofounder, Christian Harvest International
Strategic Prayer Apostolic Network
International Freedom Group
Transformational Alliance Partnership
Christian Harvest Training Center

FOREWORD

We knew it all along! This book is a great, new, exciting, and groundbreaking contribution to the field of deliverance from demonic bondages. Every deliverance minister needs a copy of this in his or her library!

I have been working in the field of deliverance for almost 40 years now, and it has been so gratifying to see people greatly helped through this ministry. I receive so many wonderful testimonies from individuals who say things such as, "I feel so very much better!" or the most common remark seems to be, "I feel so much lighter, like some sort of a weight has been lifted."

Jareb and Petra Nott have carefully collected and interpreted the scientific data that explains these good feelings after deliverance has occurred. They start by explaining how a demon can attach itself to an individual's emotions, causing great discomfort and harm to that person, and how to get rid of that hitchhiking demonic being. A demon must have a reason to attach itself to a person's emotions, and a very long list of the most common ways this occurs is outlined. The carefully crafted prayers of renunciation at the end of the book suggested for use during a deliverance session are very helpful tools.

But what is it that scientifically occurs when an individual is delivered from the demonic bondages of things such as unforgiveness, fear, anger, hatred, rejection, or a myriad of other very negative emotions? That individual has testified to the fact that something definitely happened in his or her body and soul, but up until now we have been unable to identify that which scientifically occurred to the various organs of the body right down to the smallest particles of which we are so "fearfully and wonderfully made."

The first inkling that I got of this appeared in a short article by Katy Koontz in the July issue of a magazine called *Arthritis Today*, page 40. The headline read "Forgiveness Heals." It was followed by the statement, "To err is human, to forgive is healing." And it went on to clearly and distinctly explain in a couple of paragraphs that forgiving an individual who has harmed you may mend a relationship, will greatly improve your physical condition, as well as lessen the pain of the person struggling with arthritis. I have used this material for years and years as I lecture on the importance of forgiving as outlined in the Holy Bible. We always knew that Jesus commanded us to forgive; as a matter of fact, it is the only portion of the very famous Lord's Prayer that Jesus repeated. The phrase used in the Lord's Prayer is "forgive us our sins as we forgive those who sin against us." He then goes on to say that if we do not forgive neither will our Father in heaven forgive us when we have need of forgiveness.

But then we discovered why Jesus instructed us to forgive. Forgiveness really helps the person feel better and healthier—in other words, forgiveness is good for your health. It not only makes you feel better in your emotions, but it improves your health as well by actually helping vital organs become stronger. A whole chapter is devoted to the scientific and scriptural evidence that has been forthcoming on this subject. I really loved the way Jareb and Petra help people in the forgiveness process, because, as we so emphatically teach, it is the *person* you are forgiving, not the awful sin they committed against you. Reconciliation does not necessarily have to occur, if it is not wise or even possible to do so. This is why so many people get hung up on forgiving—they think that the sin needs to be forgiven, when we encourage the person to separate out the individual from the sin or crime and forgive the person for allowing satan to use him or her to do the harm. Sometimes a person has to choose to forgive, and the damage has been so horrible that only Jesus can help them forgive.

Jareb and Petra Nott have taken the time to pull together a tremendous amount of scientific evidence that proves that—yes, indeed—something wonderful has happened in the very DNA of a person who has gone through a complete deliverance experience. A measure of physical healing occurs when the demon that has attached itself to an emotion such as unforgiveness, rejection, fear, anger, or the like is dispatched and emotional healing immediately takes place. Great detail is given on the scientific evidence that has been uncovered and what actually occurs, and it is astounding! Science is finally catching up with Scripture and giving us a reasonable explanation that encourages us to keep on preaching and teaching what the Bible says. We always knew that it was God's will to forgive, for example, but we never had the scientific evidence as to how healthy it is. It literally changes the

DNA in our organs and bodies for the better. You will love the chapter on epigenetics.

I thoroughly enjoyed the chapter on meditation. We have been instructed in God's word also that we should meditate on Scripture and things pertaining thereto. A clear outline as to a suggested method for starters is provided and will be greatly appreciated by those who are just starting out on a journey of meditation.

DORIS M. WAGNER
Co-founder of the International Society
of Deliverance Ministers

CHAPTER ONE

INTRODUCTION

When healing occurs in your emotions or your thought patterns, that healing will also manifest in some way, shape, or form in your physical body. When a demonic spirit detaches from a person, the body will respond with healing and new vitality. Like a beach ball that has been held underwater, when the weight of oppression is removed it bounds back to the surface, back to its natural state of buoyancy where it should have been all along. It may sound like an outrageous claim, but it is this truth—one I've observed repeatedly and experienced myself—that prompted the writing of this book.

One such case occurred in the early days of our training in deliverance. The young woman who had requested prayer was miserable. Her severe stomach pain had onset suddenly and inexplicably several months earlier. She had been to the doctor many times, had tried medications, adjustments in her diet, and more—all to no avail. She was a student and had missed so many classes due to the pain that she was in danger of not graduating on time. She was also a believer and her friends, family, and church members had all been praying faithfully for her physical healing, but that did not seem to be having any impact. She was growing weary and fearful. We were friends of the family and I had volunteered to pray for her. Yes, many others had prayed already, but they had been praying for healing in her physiology from natural causes. I felt a deep stirring that this was a spiritual issue, and God was going to deal with it on a spiritual level. As she sat in front of us, we asked the Holy Spirit for revelation as to the root cause of the issue. Her parents were there with us, and they began to get revelation as well—trauma during her birth, generational issues in the family, and all of it culminating and being activated as she was about to move into adulthood and into her own calling. We led her through simple prayers breaking off all of these demonic attachments and asking for healing in her mind and emotions from all trauma either experienced or inherited. We also had her repent for generational sin on behalf of her family line. She could feel something moving around in her stomach as she spoke those words, and upon us pressing the issue and commanding it to leave, she finally felt the demonic spirit detach completely. She was in peace. The pain never returned, and she was able to graduate on time. In this case, physical pain had a spiritual root requiring spiritual healing.

Many other clients come to our ministry looking for spiritual and emotional healing only and are quite surprised when physical healing follows; they did not realize the connection and so did not anticipate any outcome in the realm of their natural health. And occasionally we have quite a different scenario, where a medical doctor or nurse will come to us for ministry because they believe it necessary to resolve some health issue in their body; they have tried everything their own profession has to offer and eventually realized if it was a purely physical cause, they should have gotten better results with standard treatments.

All of this leads us back to the main point: when we minister, we expect to see healing in your body. That healing may be instantaneous and noticeable, or it may be a process of incremental adjustments in your genetic code, your microbiome, your neural pathways, your hormones, your immune system, etc., until it finally becomes evident to you outwardly. Whether quickly or slowly, dramatically or quietly, a shift toward physical health is the inevitable result of spiritual freedom.

This is indeed a strange idea to those of us living in modern, science-driven culture. We have been taught to compartmentalize; mental health is in one box, emotional health is in a different container, physical health in yet a different box, and spiritual health is in a bucket in the corner, if it exists at all. Believing ourselves to be scientific and superior, modern society imagines that these things never touch or "cross-contaminate." Conventional wisdom advises people to see a counselor or life coach for emotional issues, a psychiatrist for mental issues, a pastor for spiritual issues, and a medical doctor for anything physical. Now each of these professions are relevant and useful and I don't intend to imply otherwise. However, there is a problem in that we often look at each facet of the human being in isolation; we attempt to bring healing to the one part we understand while ignoring the others, and this is like plugging one hole in a sinking boat but leaving several other holes unchecked. We must begin with the understanding that these different facets of ourselves are not in neat, sterile little compartments. In fact, while they certainly can "cross-contaminate" when one area is damaged, the good news is they also "cross-pollinate" when one area moves into a place of health.

Another piece of good news is that the old paradigm of compartmentalism is beginning to unravel, and ironically this is due in large part to scientific research! Slowly but surely, scientists find connections between our emotional state and our mental health, between our mental health and our physical health, between what we think and say and our genetic expression, between what we eat and the state of our emotions, between physical and emotional pain, and on it goes. This integrative understanding has always been the biblical view of health, and now, thousands of years later, modern human knowledge begins to see the evidence for these principles and finally accept them as fact.

Hearing about these discoveries should captivate us all with God's design for healing! While I am not a scientist, I am dedicated to being a lifelong learner. There is something that resonates deep within my heart when I read, *"It is the glory of God to conceal a matter; to search out a matter is the glory of kings."* (Prov. 25:2). Thus, I have always been fascinated by reading about scientific discoveries. At its core, the pursuit of science is an endeavor to increase humankind's body of knowledge regarding the workings of creation. As believers, we have the additional and deeper motive that knowing more of creation gives us a better understanding of the Creator Himself. The inherent flaw of science is that it only pursues knowledge of the physical realm, and indeed it is forever bound by that limitation because humankind cannot on a regular or consistent basis observe the spirit realm. Knowing our limitations, the Holy Spirit is our teacher to help us connect the dots between the "seen" and the "unseen." And when the Holy Spirit begins making those connections, it feels like they pop up at every turn. Out of mere curiosity (or so I might have thought at the time), I would read an article on a new scientific theory or discovery and suddenly realize it mirrored a spiritual understanding I had learned from the Bible, or something the Holy Spirit had often led us to do while ministering. It was amazing how many science-to-spirit parallels I continually "stumbled across." Things I had always taken as true by faith were now showing up in peer-reviewed studies in scientific journals. We began using that knowledge in ministry to fine-tune our methods and often to explain to our clients a new take on scriptures they had previously thought were just allegory.

In explaining the purpose of this book, it is also useful to explain what it is not.

This book is not an attempt to validate scripture. It is always exciting when science manages to catch up with scripture a tiny bit more, as this helps us understand on a more technical level principles that God has always presented as true. However, scripture requires no validation, and indeed, if you were to go down that path, you would never reach a conclusion, as the mysteries contained in God's word are multi-dimensional and endless.

Also, as mentioned above, science is limited to human observations of the physical world; therefore, it can never be used to "prove" or, conversely, to "disprove" spiritual phenomena. Rather, I believe scripture because I have encountered the one true God. I have personally been transformed by His love, have assurance of salvation due to His sacrifice, and based on that trust I take

His written word as wholly true and inerrant. Essentially, I believe it based on a trusting relationship with my heavenly Father, and based on a lifetime of living it out and finding it to be accurate and reliable in every situation.

This book is not an attempt to turn deliverance into a purely cerebral undertaking or scientific method. In fact, we have come to realize that while there are principles of deliverance that are true, and there are certainly some best practices, each ministry receiver is unique, and each deliverance minister is unique, so methods can differ and still be effective. There is no single cut-and-dry method that we can copy by rote each time. Our best example of this is in the many recorded miracles of Jesus; we do not see where He ever performed a healing exactly the same way twice. As humans, we want to press the "easy button," to have someone give us a three-step process that will always work without fail. We would prefer to say, "Everyone who has leprosy should travel to the Jordan river and dip seven times like Naaman," or, "When praying for a blind person, you should always spit in the dirt and rub the resulting mud in the person's eyes, because that is how Jesus healed the blind man." That would be so easy! We could print a handbook of precise methods for all ministers to follow in any given situation, and we would have no further need for training or study. But no, we see in scripture that these situations, and their solutions, were unique. Each person has a different story; even two people who came through very similar trauma may have different points of wounding where they are stuck, different lies they believe, and need to experience healing in different ways. Additionally, I have come to believe that God is not a huge fan of "formulas" in ministry, partly because they can be so impotent, but also because His children have a long history of substituting formula for relationship (this is the essence of "religion"). Once we have our set way of doing things, it easily slips into a type of religious ceremony or ritual wherein we rely on our own power, ability, understanding, and actions, believing that repetition will bring about a specific result. How much better it is to seek God on behalf of each person! To listen to the Holy Spirit. The only "methodology" that will never fail us is to only say what we hear the Father saying and only do what we see Him doing.

With that said, where does science come in? If we can follow God's instructions and be effective, then why is understanding needed? Science is useful because it increases our understanding of what God asks us to do, and because the more we understand about creation, the more revelation we have about the Creator Himself. Many of us as schoolkids found we learned much better when we understood the "why" behind the rules of any particular discipline, and the best teachers are able to convey those principles that are at work behind the scenes. This enables the student to better remember and apply the information and to have a true appreciation for the workings of that subject. It helps the student avoid mistakes in the future and make better decisions when engaging in that discipline.

This book is not an attempt to link spiritual causality to every physical ailment. In fact, I do not believe that every physical problem has a root spiritual cause. Sometimes an accident is just an accident. We can be exposed to harmful chemicals, side effects of medications, and a myriad of naturally occurring harms. However, when a physical issue is particularly traumatic or goes on long term, it can begin to wreak havoc on a person in their soul realm. Pain has a way of opening the door to depression, anger, bitterness, and hope deferred. Conversely, we know that emotional wounds and demonic attachments can indeed be the cause of physical pain and suffering. On this note I believe two things: 1) the Holy Spirit can and will reveal and deal with the root cause or entry point of pain in the body or soul realm, and 2) it is a waste of time to argue about which came first, the chicken or the egg. When both the body and the soul need healing, then the person should aim to bring healing to both simultaneously! Seek out what is needed in the realm of health, wellness, and medicine (under God's guidance), while also seeking out healing in your emotions and breaking off all demonic attachments, which will also resonate through and have a beneficial impact on your physical body.

This book is about increasing our understanding of how the soul and the body both sustain injury together, and heal together, and how the physical part of that equation is actually observable and quantifiable. It is about appropriating, under the guidance of the Holy Spirit, the provision for freedom that Jesus made on the cross. It is about partnering with God to bring healing of emotional wounds so that the enemy can no longer leverage those wounds against us. It is about breaking off demonic strongholds. It is recognizing deliverance as a spiritual work so powerful that it affects the totality of the person including their physical body. The technical understanding we gain through science is valuable because it helps us pray with more specificity and helps us to envision what is happening inside our bodies when we pray. (And that imagining is truly a powerful component of faith and physical healing, but more on that later!)

The concepts contained in this book are for every believer in Jesus to utilize under His guidance. While those who do not know Jesus as their Savior will still learn and benefit to a small degree, the truth is that apart from Him, we can do nothing (see John 15:5). Many individuals will be able to leverage this knowledge, pray through the prayers herein, and find total freedom through a ministry team of just themselves and the Holy Spirit! Others may find they need more support, and in those cases we urge those people to seek out a reputable deliverance ministry and submit to a process of prayer with a team of trained and compassionate believers.

Deliverance ministers can benefit greatly by utilizing the instructions and prayers contained in this book with their clients. Those of us who do this type of ministry are approached by people who have pain on every level—emotional, physical, mental, and spiritual. Scripture tells us that *"An intelligent heart acquires knowledge, and the ear of the wise seeks knowledge"* (Prov. 18:15 ESV), and we do well to heed that advice when dealing with the delicate situation of a person who is in torment. It is one thing to have tools; it is a better thing to have a comprehensive understanding of the workings of those tools, how and why they are effective, and how to wield them with care and expertise. We should always be expanding our understanding of how to partner with God in healing, as this preparation strengthens us to be used of Him in greater ways during ministry. If I have trained my body to walk many miles, then God can send me on longer journeys; if I have trained my mind and spirit to partner with Him in healing, then He can use me in greater measure as a conduit for His healing power to flow into others.

Other types of ministers can greatly benefit from this knowledge as well—healing ministers, counselors, pastors, parents, and believers who work in the health industry.

I have a background in corporate training, through which I became familiar with the industry mantra that "telling isn't training." In other words, my job back then was to teach you how to perform a task or improve your ability to do so in some way, not to merely throw information at you so that you could memorize it long enough to pass a test or sound more intelligent.

Let's imagine a scenario where I am teaching a class how to bake chocolate chip cookies. I might begin with a monologue on the importance of family connection, how little moments like baking together become the stuff memories are made of down the road. I might talk about how sitting down with your children for a helping of milk and cookies gives them a chance to relax, bond with you, and share what is on their hearts. All of that might motivate you a great deal, but what if we left it at that? What if you had no cooking experience whatsoever, and I never actually told you *how* to bake those cookies? What if I didn't give you a list of ingredients or any instructions on the proper order in which to mix them, the temperature of the oven, or the baking time? I might have inspired you that baking cookies is a great idea, but in the end you would get home to your own kitchen and think, "Wait, how exactly am I supposed to get started?" You would be left to your own devices to figure out the process. And while some people are self-motivated enough to look up the details they need and research how to carry them out effectively, many more become frustrated at their lack of ability to implement and fizzle out. They move on, never putting into practice the thing that originally sparked their enthusiasm. It is my belief that, too often, we as teachers in the body of Christ approach biblical instruction in this way. We provide emotional or even mental stimulation but leave people with no resulting action items to implement, no mechanism by which to bring change to their lives and the world around them.

Thus, while it is my hope that this book will be inspirational, revelatory, and uplifting, I want those qualities to be a springboard into action. We need to build a bridge from inspiration over to practical application so that the excitement does not burn out like a sparkler and fade into distant memory. Good training will either show you "how" or will connect you to resources that will provide that part of the equation.

In this book, it is my highest goal to close that gap between revelation and activation! I don't want to merely stimulate your intellectual side with fascinating information from the front lines of science and get your faith engines revved up by drawing a line from that over to God being a really awesome Creator. No, I want to go a step further and give you real-world application homework for every single teaching in this book. Ideally, a trainer will sit down with every single student, walk them through the steps, make them practice, and give them real-time feedback—put them behind the wheel for a test drive, so to speak. But as it is not possible for me to sit down with each of you, I am instead including in this book tools you can utilize to put your newfound knowledge into practice!

Ultimately, the goals are for you to:

- Understand that your body and soul are not compartmentalized, but synergistic—what affects one affects the other;
- Understand the effects that sin, both personal and generational, have on your whole being;
- Understand the effects of demonic oppression on the mind, body, and emotions;
- Understand the authority you have in Christ to invoke His power for healing in your mind, body, and emotions;
- Understand the "how" behind wielding that authority—to know what tools you have and how to use them well;
- Understand, expect, and experience the phenomenon of physical healing as a result of spiritual healing.

God will make the healing happen in the right timing, at the right speed, and in the right order for each individual. Our job is to utilize His design for our body, soul, and spirit to work together toward health. We must also believe in His supernatural intervention. We must believe that He is able to heal, He is willing to heal, and we must hear His voice for each next step and partner with His instructions. It is my prayer that the following pages will help you along that journey!

CHAPTER TWO

PHYSICAL FREEDOM THROUGH SPIRITUAL DELIVERANCE

What I am about to say may sound like a stretch of reality. These statements may even conflict with what you currently know about the ministry of deliverance. Allow these revelations to challenge you and enlarge your understanding of the ministry of biblical deliverance. For anyone who has been raised in the church, deliverance as a topic of ministry is either:

A. Given a general overview concerning Jesus' ministry. You are likely familiar with the demoniac where Jesus allowed Legion to enter a herd of pigs. Perhaps treating it like it's a fascinating true story that reads like fiction in some ways.

B. Not discussed or addressed in the church. Anyone who was seen or heard manifesting was removed from the congregation and talk of demons was prohibited.

C. It was taught and discussed, and members of the church were taught to deal with demonic manifestations.

D. Manifestations were brought to the front and addressed by the elders for the congregation to hear and witness.

Whatever your level of understanding is, the next few statements will either challenge or resonate with you; my desire is that they will cause you to ask questions concerning the nature of deliverance and the methods currently used by deliverance ministries all over the world.

After ministering for more than a decade, I have learned many different methods concerning deliverance. Some techniques work and some do not. But when we welcome the Holy Spirit and allow Him to lead the experience, He always shows up to gently bring healing and freedom from demonic torment. One area that always concerned me was the fact that receiving freedom from demonic oppression was only part of the total healing package that we offered to people in need. We are made of three parts: spirit, soul, and body. Historically and generally concerning the church, deliverance ministry addressed the spirit and the soul through the casting out of demons. Anything dealing with the body was referred to as a "healing ministry." Occasionally we would be fortunate enough to have someone on the team who operated in the gift of healing as well. Having that convenience made for an easy referral when physical healing was necessary. I thank God for those whose primary gift is healing; they are vital to the body of Christ. However, why do deliverance ministers often feel inadequate to handle issues of a physical nature? I believe it is because we as a church have drawn a line between the spiritual and the physical where healing is concerned. We have believed that physical healing needs require a different gift set and must be handled differently.

This book was written to highlight truth and show that our current understanding of deliverance ministry may need a course correction, perhaps even a reset. Biblically we never see Jesus draw a line between healing the demonized and the physically afflicted. He healed them together, at the same time! *Therefore, we can confidently state that all deliverance ministry can and should be accompanied by some form of physical healing!* That is a bold statement, and we will soon see further biblical proof of this statement as well. Furthermore, this book will show through biblical example, testimony, and scientific evidence that physical healing and deliverance go hand in hand every single time.

The Bible tells us in First Corinthians 3:11, "*For no one can lay any foundation other than the one already laid, which is Jesus Christ.*" All things pertaining to deliverance ministry must begin and end with Jesus, the example He gave, and the revelation that He continues to give us as we pursue Him. What follows are several biblical confirmations concerning:

1. Our authority as believers
2. The deliverance and healing model presented by Jesus Himself as He ministered deliverance regularly

Deliverance ministry is not a gift or a handy tool that is found exclusively in the toolbox of those who are primarily called to be "deliverance ministers." Rather, the role of deliverance is an assignment for *all* who call themselves believers and, as a result, disciples of Jesus.

All Authority

Jesus summoned His twelve disciples and gave them authority and power over unclean spirits, to cast them out, and to heal every kind of disease and every kind of sickness (Matthew 10:1 AMP).

In this passage, Jesus is modeling an impartation of power and authority to His disciples, the body of believers who follow Him. This event is no small prayer or spiritual act. Jesus summoned the disciples. He recognized the need for deliverance and healing will increase and people will need freedom. Notice that He did not bestow new gifts on them. He did not tell some of the disciples that they were to handle the demonized, while others were to handle the sick and diseased. No, Jesus mantled each of them with power and authority to execute judgment and justice over demons, sickness, and disease. It was all inclusive. There is freedom here for all believers to operate in the power granted by Jesus to be ministers of complete and thorough healing. Let's keep looking.

Jesus Healed All Who Were Demon Possessed

Jesus went throughout Galilee, teaching in their synagogues, proclaiming the good news of the kingdom, and healing every disease and sickness among the people. News about him spread all over Syria, and people brought to him all who were ill with various diseases, those suffering severe pain, the demon-possessed, those having seizures, and the paralyzed; and he healed them (Matthew 4:23–24).

Here we clearly see Jesus modeling and demonstrating the deliverance and healing method. People who were demonized and who needed healing came to see Him. Jesus simply healed them all. Once again, we do not see a separation—no queuing for a qualified deliverance minister to help them. Where was the triaging of people to be whisked away to prevent commotion and distraction? All were welcome and all were healed together because affliction of either the spirit, the soul, or the body is still an affliction that requires healing. I'm not suggesting that demons be allowed to distract and cause disruption. On the contrary, believers should be equipped to effectively handle these situations by forbidding (binding) demonic manifestations so that the person can receive ministry without becoming a distraction from the corporate goal God has for the public gathering. Likewise, demons must not be allowed to distract ministry during private ministry either. This is why the tools of binding (forbidding) and loosing (permitting) were given to all believers. Make note of the deliverance tools in your spiritual arsenal. Use these tools with confidence and the guidance of the Holy Spirit. Then you will see freedom come in power.

Blind and Mute

Then they brought him a demon-possessed man who was blind and mute, and Jesus healed him, so that he could both talk and see (Matthew 12:22).

In all of these examples, Jesus provides the undisputed model of deliverance ministry—healing and deliverance working together. This man received physical healing as well as freedom from his demonic oppression. That is our model!

The Demonized Boy

The next day, when they came down from the mountain, a large crowd met him. A man in the crowd called out, "Teacher, I beg you to look at my son, for he is my only child. A spirit seizes him and he suddenly screams; it throws him into convulsions so that he foams at the mouth. It scarcely ever leaves him and is destroying him. I begged your disciples to drive it out, but they could not." "You unbelieving and perverse generation," Jesus replied, "how long shall I stay with you and put up with you? Bring your son here." Even while the boy was coming, the demon threw him to the ground in a convulsion. But Jesus rebuked the impure spirit, healed the boy and gave him back to his father. And they were all amazed at the greatness of God (Luke 9:37–43).

Once again, we see Jesus presented with a demonized and tormented individual. It is my belief that this child's father or family was involved in sin that allowed the demon to enter and establish itself in the family. In this case the man's child was the victim of an impure familiar spirit. Scripture does not elaborate, but we know that unconfessed and unrepentant sin creates an open door for the enemy to come right in and bind itself to the family bloodline.

Jesus provides our example for deliverance ministry. He also provides us the revelation necessary to continue our growth and do the greater works. Some of the concepts within this book are revelation from God concerning deliverance ministry. The overarching goal will always be to bring glory to God through the abundant use and demonstration of our gifts as deliverance ministers—to ultimately to see the demonized, bound, and tormented set free from captivity, bondage, and slavery.

Not All Issues Are Demonic: Balance Is Key

Have you ever done something and immediately regretted it? I (Jareb) have a sister five years younger than me. When we were very young I would antagonize her, and she would get riled up and chase me out of her frustration. I loved it and would taunt her just to see her get mad. On one occasion I taunted her as usual, only this time I began to chase her. I was older and faster and she was never able to outrun me. But on this occasion as I was chasing her outside, she ran into the house and quickly closed the glass door behind her. I continued to run, and as the door closed I reached out to push my way into the house after her and my arm went right through the glass door. I'll spare you the details, but it was a pretty impressive-looking crime scene. I had cut my radial artery in two places on my arm and was quickly rushed to the emergency room for care. Looking back on that experience nearly forty years later, I can tell you that I did not make a wise decision. That lack of wisdom on my part was caused by my own stubborn, competitive, immature desire to win.

In yet another example, in 1996 I visited Russia with a group of Christian leaders. During this visit we took the opportunity to visit local landmarks and see the sights. As we were walking down a path en route to our next stop, I suddenly found myself tumbling down an open manhole! The manhole cover was partially removed, and as I blindly stepped on it the cover flipped, and I went down the hole. Thankfully a fair amount of wooden scaffolding broke my fall on the way down to the bottom. I was sore and embarrassed, but in good shape considering the dramatic experience. I was hoisted out of the hole and proceeded on toward my destination just fine.

The point of these stories is to illustrate that I was not oppressed with a demon who caused me to make these mistakes. There was no demon waiting to push me into that hole, nor was there a demon waiting to ensure that I lacerated my arm. I am also not saying that we must make terrible mistakes before we learn our lessons. That is why the book of Proverbs was written. Likewise, if you are caught speeding it's likely not because you have a speed demon attached to you. Paul puts it this way in Galatians 5:13:

> For you, brethren, were [indeed] called to freedom; only [do not let your] freedom be an incentive to your flesh and an opportunity or excuse [for selfishness], but through love you should serve one another (AMPC).

We must realize that the choices we make have consequences. We do not have immunity or absolution from the consequences of our actions. We have a merciful God, a loving Father who will never send us away; He will never leave (unfasten) us or forsake (abandon) us. One of the ugly truths of our consequences is that sometimes our choices and mistakes lead to open doors for the enemy to come in, torment, and even demonize. Watching the wrong things on TV, accessing the wrong websites on our phone, unhealthy relationships, and participation in ungodly actions open doors and create an environment where demons have an open door to walk right in and make themselves comfortable.

One of the things we will discuss in-depth later in this book is the effect our misdeeds have on our DNA and our physical bodies. When I sliced my radial artery, my DNA was marked with the trauma of that experience. That trauma was literally written into the DNA and replicated in every single cell of my body. These marks on our DNA can surface later in life as infirmities, fears, phobias, and mental health concerns.

But God! The truth is that we do not have to be bound any longer by the mistakes of our past. Every door the enemy walked through can be closed. Every cell and all DNA within your body can receive miraculous healing that will manifest outwardly. The Bible says in Romans 12:2, *"Be transformed by the renewing of your mind."* It goes on to say in Proverbs 23:7, *"For as he thinks in his heart, so is he"* (AMP).

One of the areas believers must take to heart is our involvement in the opening of doors to the enemy. Each time we willingly and knowingly sin we open ourselves for demonic attack. For example, evil and lustful images appear in front of us frequently—some are unavoidable. It is not the first innocent glance that is the issue; it's the second and subsequent glances that move us from innocence to willing participation with evil. At that moment, we've opened a door and invited the enemy in to rent-free space in our minds. Another example would be choosing to watch a TV show where the plot revolves around witchcraft and casting spells. In this example we have opened a couple doors to the enemy. First, your eyes are direct entry points to your mind and your soul. By watching, you have shown the demonic realm an open door into your life. The next door opened is to your home. The entertainment center in your home is both a spiritual and worldly portal into your home. Allowing demonic entertainment is allowing, even inviting that spirit to invade your home as well. I've worked with too many people who are oppressed as a direct result of what they allowed into the home through their television. Think about the children in your home; even if they do not see the content directly, if you are watching demonic, occult, horror, sexual, or witchcraft entertainment, then you are welcoming those spirits into the atmosphere you share with your family, children, guests, and anyone else who comes into your home. Instead, cultivate an atmosphere of God's presence. Wouldn't it be preferable to saturate our families, children, and guests with the glory of God instead?

One of the many messages we will impart in this book is that as believers, we have the God-given power to literally heal our physical and spiritual bodies using the words in our mouth and the thoughts in our mind. This healing requires our alignment with truth and with what God says about us. If we were made to be more than conquerors, why do we let infirmity, disease, and demonic torment continue to invade the holy temples of our bodies? This book will demonstrate how you can partner with the power of God to drive demons out and heal your body from all infirmity, even if you have willingly partnered with it in your past.

All Deliverance Is Accompanied by Physical Healing

I've provided scriptural evidence that physical healing accompanies the ministry of deliverance. Traditional deliverance ministry is truly a God-send to those in demonic captivity. Yet God has provided revelation that moves us beyond traditional deliverance ministry, and our desire is for this book to be a catalyst of that knowledge. In Matthew 10:1 Jesus called His disciples into a private meeting. During this meeting, Jesus imparted to them both power and authority over demonic spirits, disease, and infirmity. Can you picture sitting in that meeting? Jesus set up the format of the meeting—it was not to be a discussion; they were not about to discuss plans for how to handle people with problems. This was a top-down message that was intended to clearly ordain them with spiritual authority and power over all things spiritual and physical. Did you ever wonder why Jesus spoke of demonic oppression and infirmity together in that meeting? I believe it was because, regardless of the definition, bondage is bondage, sickness is sickness, and infirmity is infirmity. They all affect the body and they all impair God's people from walking in their destiny. Jesus knew He needed ambassadors of His to carry power and authority, so that when used properly it could assist all His followers through the rest of history toward walking in their true identities. The truth is the disciples in that meeting were the very first ordained and commissioned deliverance ministers. They were released to render judgment on every demonic assignment in the earth.

Today, you and I also represent the kingdom as God's ambassadors. We are deliverance ministers of freedom. We have been commissioned to go into the world, preaching, teaching, healing the sick, and casting out demons.

From a scientific perspective, the demons attacking God's people know they have access through our thoughts. This is why the Bible tells us to "be transformed by the renewing of our mind." The demonic realm knows this, and they try very hard to influence us through our thoughts. Scientifically speaking, our thoughts are physical objects, they are observable, and each one of them impacts every one of the trillions of cells within our bodies. So if the enemy can invade our thought life, then our physical bodies will react in kind. Dr. Bruce Lipton who specializes in cell biology says this:

> Your thoughts are things. They are actual proteins called neurotransmitters, serotonin, dopamine, adrenaline which attach to cell membranes and cause your genes to express themselves. And that expression, that gene expression is inheritable over the next few generations. So, you are not a victim of your genes, you have some control over how they are expressed.[1]

One thing that is vital to Christian growth is the enormity and responsibility of the great commission. For some it means traveling and evangelizing the world with the good news of the gospel. However, it is more than that. As an ordained and commissioned deliverance minister I see it as a calling to all believers as needed in their daily lives. Not just a nice thing to do, but a must do. Jesus did not say, "Some of you will heal infirmities, and some of you will cast out demons." No, He commissioned every believer for the entire package. We are to be known as universal deliverance ministers. We do it all!

Starting now, let's begin to acknowledge the power and authority we carry as believers in Jesus to change lives and minister identity. One caveat—this power and authority are not to be a plaque on the wall as an acknowledgment of our credentials. We are sons and daughters of the King. True sons and daughters don't boast of their abilities. However, as believers in Jesus we must acknowledge and declare over ourselves the truth that we have this power and authority. Only then can it be used to bring glory to God, set the captives free, and to literally heal the brokenhearted.

NOTE

1. Dr. Ron Ehrlich, "Dr. Bruce Lipton – A New Hope: Epigenetics and the Subconscious Mind," Unstress with Dr. Ron Ehrlich, accessed June 21, 2021, https://drronehrlich.com/dr-bruce -lipton-a-new -hope-epigenetics-and-the-subconscious-mind-2.

CHAPTER THREE

EPIGENETICS, DNA, AND DEMONS

You shall not make for yourself an image in the form of anything in heaven above or on the earth beneath or in the waters below. You shall not bow down to them or worship them; for I, the Lord your God, am a jealous God, punishing the children for the sin of the parents to the third and fourth generation of those who hate me, but showing love to a thousand generations of those who love me and keep my commandments (Deuteronomy 5:8–10).

Generational Bondage and Inheritance

This book is not written to debate the sovereignty of God. I will state emphatically that God does not bestow suffering on His children. We are not predestined for suffering, and the doctrine of determinism is unscriptural.

Having said that, let's look at the scientific logic that explains why iniquity can pass down generationally. Science is remarkable because it can unknowingly confirm what we've believed based on scripture for more than two thousand years, and help to provide practical insight into many of our common questions, such as: How does iniquity pass down generationally? Does it happen to everyone? Can generational bloodline curses be broken? What about my children who are already born? Is it too late for them if they have already been handed down negative things through our bloodline? First, let's understand God's desire for us as His children.

Exhibit A

> *For you created my inmost being; you knit me together in my mother's womb. I praise you because I am fearfully and wonderfully made; your works are wonderful, I know that full well. My frame was not hidden from you when I was made in the secret place, when I was woven together in the depths of the earth. Your eyes saw my unformed body; all the days ordained for me were written in your book before one of them came to be* (Psalm 139:13–16).

You are fearfully and wonderfully made! God does not make mistakes, nor does He write suffering and pain into your book. Verse 17 makes this clear where it states, *"How precious are your thoughts."*

Exhibit B

> *"For I know the plans I have for you,"* declares the Lord, *"plans to prosper you and not to harm you, plans to give you hope and a future"* (Jeremiah 29:11).

Although this verse was addressing the nation of Israel, I believe that all who come to salvation in Jesus are adopted into God's family, and thus are beneficiaries. Further, I believe the "plans" mentioned here refer to the "days ordained" written in your heavenly book in the first scripture above. God's desire for His children is for us to live a life full of joy and relationship with Him. However, we are not absolved from making our own choices. It is these choices that determine what will pass down generationally. We will see that curses pass down generationally, but what about blessings?

Generational Blessings

For he knows how we are formed, he remembers that we are dust. The life of mortals is like grass, they flourish like a flower of the field; the wind blows over it and it is gone, and its place remembers it no more. But from everlasting to everlasting the Lord's love is with those who fear him, and his righteousness with their children's children (Psalm 103:14–17).

In Genesis 12:3, God is speaking to Abram, setting him on his journey, and He tells Abram that all generations will be blessed through his obedience: *"I will bless those who bless you, and whoever curses you I will curse; and all peoples on earth will be blessed through you"* (Gen. 12:3). The principle I am introducing here is that God established a spiritual pipeline for the express purpose of passing down blessings through family bloodlines, both spiritually and physically. More on that thought in a moment. The Bible contains hundreds of references to blessings and the passing on of them generationally. Sadly, as a result of the fall in the garden this pipeline was compromised, and the enemy uses it to carry bloodline curses. I am going to explain how blessings and curses travel through our generations. The good news is that we have victory over the plans of the enemy to stop the flow of curses and reset the pipeline for blessings in our lives and the lives of our families.

Epigenetic Markers

Before we continue let me address the term *epigenetics*. I will use this term throughout this book and you will no doubt hear it more now that you are aware of the research.

Epigenetics is a relatively new way of understanding the building blocks of DNA. Until very recently, molecular biology has held to a central dogma that you are the result of your DNA and nothing can change the cards you have been dealt in life.

Science has now adapted to a new understanding of how DNA works. Epigenetics changes what we know about DNA and genetic inheritance through the bloodline.

    a.   The fact is that your DNA is not your destiny.

    b.   With the Holy Spirit, you have the power to change your destiny!

Epigenetics is the study of how your behaviors and environment can cause changes that affect the way your genes work. Unlike genetic changes, epigenetic changes are reversible.[1]

Epigenetics is a compound word which brings new light to how we look at our DNA.

Today, the most common definition of the word is a back-translation of "epi" (upon, above, beyond) and "genetic" (DNA sequence), referring to a layer of information that exists beyond that encoded in the DNA sequence, thereby making the genome function distinctively in different cell types.[2]

The epigenome or "epigenetic marks" sit on top of the genome (the cell and everything contained within) and influence changes to your genes, essentially telling them to turn on or turn off.

We have been led to believe that our genes determine the character of our lives, yet new research surprisingly reveals that it is the character of our lives that controls our genes. Rather than being victims of our heredity, we are actually masters of our genome.[3]

God has given us the freedom to command our own lives and bodies through His gift of free will. Scripture tells us on many occasions to "choose" for ourselves.

But if serving the Lord seems undesirable to you, then choose for yourselves this day whom you will serve, whether the gods your ancestors served beyond the Euphrates, or the gods of the Amorites, in whose land you are living. But as for me and my household, we will serve the Lord (Joshua 24:15).

As we saw in Psalm 139:16, each person has a book penned by God Himself, which contains His perfect will for our lives. But we can and often do choose not to open it, read what is inside, and bring our actions into agreement with what is written.

The verse above in Joshua is a beautiful example of the generational impact of our choices. God says, "Choose to follow Me or accept the generational curses in your ancestral bloodlines by worshiping false gods."

Each one of these choices we make leaves an imprint or a mark on our DNA that is passed down the family bloodline. The implication here is that each of us must decide to reverse the curse and detach ourselves from the generational iniquity within our bloodlines.

Passed to the Third and Fourth Generation

The following quote from the University of Utah, Genetic Science Learning Center had this to say:

> We used to think that a new embryo's epigenome was completely erased and rebuilt from scratch. But this isn't completely true. Some epigenetic tags remain in place as genetic information passes from generation to generation, a process called epigenetic inheritance.[4]

In other words, our genes are not purified and reset with each generation. Our life experiences, traumas, phobias, and even smell aversions are potentially passed down up to four generations. The National Institute of Health issued the following finding in a report on epigenetics:

> Most epigenetic modification, by whatever mechanism, is believed to be erased with each new generation.... However, one of the more startling reports published in 2005 challenges this belief and

suggests that epigenetic changes may endure in at least four subsequent generations of organisms.[5]

This statement is remarkable because of how it aligns with scripture.

> *You shall not bow down to them or worship them; for I, the Lord your God, am a jealous God, punishing the children for the sin of the parents to the third and fourth generation of those who hate me* (Deuteronomy 5:9).
>
> *You shall not make for yourself an image in the form of anything in heaven above or on the earth beneath or in the waters below. You shall not bow down to them or worship them; for I, the Lord your God, am a jealous God, punishing the children for the sin of the parents to the third and fourth generation of those who hate me* (Exodus 20:4–5).

We are beginning to understand the reality of how generational curses have the power to destroy lives, and this cannot be overstated. The Bible is always accurate, and the science is a confirmation. For example, the media reported that during the attack on 9/11, roughly 1,700 pregnant women were directly affected by the attack and aftermath. Reports also show that these women were affected by PTSD symptoms and that their newborn children also demonstrated PTSD symptoms. Additionally, these children were found to have inherited their mother's experiences from that day in the form of phobias, fears, and trauma responses. What this means is that the trauma was marked on the mother's DNA and subsequently the child's DNA through epigenetic mechanisms.[6]

If we do not intentionally cleanse our bloodline of generational curses, the potential for generational iniquity exists for up to four generations and possibly even more. This is stated by scripture and backed up by science as well. We don't need science to confirm what scripture tells us, but it sure is exciting when that happens.

Let me share an example of how this has appeared in deliverance ministry. I once ministered to a man who lived a life of anxiety, fear, and depression. Our interview and preliminary counseling session revealed that his life did not bear the telltale signs consistent with depression, worry, and fear. We began to minister with him. Through discernment and partnering with the Holy Spirit, we were able to determine that not only were these strongholds and manifestations not directly his, but they were also present with his grandparents and his parents. Knowing these traits were passed down generationally, we understood them to be familiar spirits and epigenetic marks on his DNA that we needed to remove through prayer. The result is a man free from generational bondage of worry, fear, and depression that was never his to carry.

This is the power of understanding the science of DNA and how the remnants of our life's choices can often pass down to our children. Here is the good news! We have been given the victory and power over these generational bloodline curses through our steadfast belief in God, intentional prayers, and participation in Holy Spirit-led deliverance ministry. We no longer need to live with the lie that we are the result of our genes. It's time to be free from that lie and receive the truth. You are meant to live free from the bondage of the past. We will have a prayer at the end of the book that will begin your healing process and reset your DNA back to the way God intended it at the moment of your creation.

How to Identify Markers: Generational or Current

This subheading might be misleading, as there is no exact formula that will identify epigenetic marks or generational curses on your bloodline. However, you can take a serious inventory of your life, ancestry, and known family history, and by coupling this with discernment from the Holy Spirit, you can determine quite a lot. There is no need to be religious about this task. Don't worry if you miss something. God can still heal unknown issues just as easily as those that are known. This simple process is meant to help you get an idea of which generational curses and epigenetic marks may be impacting your life.

Begin by taking inventory of any areas of your life where you currently or have in the past struggled with any of the following areas. Start by journaling your involvement with:

1. Fear, including phobias
2. Rejection
3. Anxiety
4. Heart problems, cardiovascular problems, high blood pressure
5. Mental health problems
6. Digestive problems
7. Respiratory problems

8. Immune system problems

9. Reproductive problems

10. High stress

11. Endocrine system dysfunction

12. Sleep disorders

13. Chronic fatigue

14. Discouragement

15. Death—physical, spiritual

16 Addictions

Next, for each issue, ask the Lord to reveal to you the moment in your life when this issue began. It might be a childhood trauma. It might be a time when you made a personal vow, and your body reacted. It may be a personal prophecy spoken over you by yourself or others. The key is to remember when each issue began and the associated memory or story. Journal these insights as well. As you journal, ask the Lord to reveal any themes or aha moments that shine a light on the true source of the pain.

This next step may involve time and research. For each issue you identified in yourself, determine to what extent each problem manifested in your family lineage. Start with your immediate parents. Then work your way back as far as you can. You will discover that patterns will emerge. You will find that the issues you are facing are actually the result of two types of generational curses. First, familiar spirits assigned to your family lineage have a mission to afflict every member of the family line and inflict as much pain and suffering as they can. They do all of this to prevent God's people from being awakened to their purpose and effectiveness in the kingdom. Second, and this piece is tied to the inherited DNA addressed earlier in this book, traumas and blessings are marked on our DNA. That DNA is passed down from generation to generation. Abraham knew the generational power of the blessing when God blessed him and all of his generations in Genesis 12:2–3:

> I will make you into a great nation, and I will bless you;
> I will make your name great, and you will be a blessing. I will bless those who bless you, and whoever curses you I will curse; and all peoples on earth will be blessed through you.

Look at this statement, "All of the people of the earth will be blessed through you." This powerful sentence establishes the portal for bloodline blessings to be passed down to all generations on the earth. It's remarkable yet so easily missed by the body of Christ. When was the last time you truly blessed someone and meant it? When was the last time you blessed yourself? Please take this opportunity to change how we think about generational inheritance. We have the power to give life to others through the gift of our Spirit-filled words.

I understand that the list you have just created is not exactly life-giving. That is precisely the intent and design of the enemy. By incapacitating God's children and taking them out of the game, satan's rule becomes that much more unchallenged. We all know the end of the book. God wins, those who believe in Jesus win, and we get to watch as satan is defeated. These curses on your life do not define you. They are not written in your kingdom book.

Now, having created your list of generational iniquity in your family lineage, it's time to deal with it. You can seek the assistance of a trained deliverance ministry to help guide you through the restoration of your bloodline. Or you can partner with the Holy Spirit and allow Him to reverse the curse. Here is a method we like to use in deliverance ministry:

For each curse you identified in your journal, repent for and renounce it on behalf of yourself and your family line. Tell all related demonic spirits to leave you immediately and to go to a dry and arid place, never to return to you or your family. Then write the opposite of each curse as a statement of blessing. Use only positive language. For example, do not say "I will *not* have anxiety." *Not* is a negative word and our bodies react to negative words even when they are said with positive intent. Instead, say, "Peace inhabits my mind, will, and emotions; I choose to have the mind of Christ that brings contentment in all areas of my life." The key with this process is to allow the Holy Spirit to help you craft your blessings. When you have finished creating your list of blessings, discard your generational curses. Begin to intentionally bless yourself and your children from the list you made. Then continue to do it daily or on a regular basis for as long as you want or need. You may discover that you may never stop blessing yourself because of the spir itual and physical benefits you will experience.

Understanding the spiritual portal and the physical DNA portals for generational blessings is a big step toward our comprehension of what God spoke over His people in Jeremiah 29:11:

> *"For I know the plans I have for you," declares the Lord,*
> *"plans to prosper you and not to harm you, plans to give*
> *you hope and a future."*

Finally, use this as an opportunity to come further into agreement with the blessing God gave Moses and Aaron when He instructed them to bless God's people:

> *The Lord said to Moses, "Tell Aaron and his sons, 'This*
> *is how you are to bless the Israelites. Say to them: "The*
> *Lord bless you and keep you; the Lord make his face shine*
> *on you and be gracious to you; the Lord turn his face*
> *toward you and give you peace"'"* (Numbers 6:22–26).

The generational curses passed down to you stand no chance against the blessings of God spoken of you and your family. Make a decision today to reverse the curse and declare that the sins of the fathers will not pass to you or your generations any longer. As my mentor in deliverance ministry, Dr. Bill Sudduth, used to say, "You have a right as a child of God to be *so free!*"

Demonic Strongholds

The spirit realm is waiting with eagerness for God's people to exercise their authority over the strongholds of satan and be victorious. Until now, satan and his demons have enjoyed free access to generational bloodlines. He's corrupted generations of family lineage through bodily systems never originally meant to pass down curses. We now have been given the knowledge of exactly how the enemy uses the mechanism of generational inheritance to keep entire generations from discovering and pursuing their kingdom purposes. A demonic stronghold is an area in our lives where the enemy has infiltrated and taken ground.

> For though we live in the world, we do not wage war as the world does. The weapons we fight with are not the weapons of the world. On the contrary, they have divine power to demolish strongholds. We demolish arguments and every pretension that sets itself up against the knowledge of God, and we take captive every thought to make it obedient to Christ (2 Corinthians 10:3–5).

Scripture tells us that we have divine power to demolish strongholds. We must choose to come out of agreement with the stronghold of the enemy in our lives. Only when we genuinely hate the evil that has enslaved us do we have the power to completely demolish and eradicate the oppressing stronghold in our entire family lineage. Scripture also tells us how this process works in verse five. "We demolish arguments and every pretension that sets itself up against the knowledge of God." Quite literally, this means to identify the lie of the enemy and demolish it with the truth! Start by meditating with the Holy Spirit. Ask Him to show you areas in your life where you have believed a lie. Then once the lie is revealed, ask the Holy Spirit to reveal the truth. The lie might be something like these statements, "I am not good enough, God cannot use me, I am broken, it is all my fault, I am to blame." Those are not life-giving statements. In fact, those beliefs become strongholds of the enemy that prevent your true identity from being revealed. Look at the second part of verse five. "We take captive every thought and make it obedient to Christ." This step is important because the enemy gets in through our thoughts and beliefs. We've identified the lie in the first half of the verse. Now we accept and partner with the truth to reverse the curse. Begin to bless yourself with the truth, taking every lie captive and replacing it with the truth of who you are as a son or daughter of the King.

Now that you've demolished the enemy's lies in your life, set your eyes on continued maintenance. It's not a once and done deal. Continuous meditation and relationship with Jesus will ensure your identity remains intact. Practically speaking, you need to *preplan* your thoughts and bring them into alignment with your kingdom identity. To understand the process, let's look in Philippians for directions on reshaping our thought life.

> *Finally, brothers and sisters, whatever is true, whatever is noble, whatever is right, whatever is pure, whatever is lovely, whatever is admirable—if anything is excellent or praiseworthy—think about such things* (Philippians 4:8).

In other words, "preplan" your thoughts, be ready for the enemy's attack, and always think on these things:

- Pure
- Right and True
- Excellent
- Praiseworthy
- Lovely
- Admirable
- Noble

Notes

1. CDC, "What is Epigenetics?" Centers for Disease Control, accessed July 2, 2021, https://www.cdc.gov/genomics/disease/epigenetics.htm.

2. John M. Greally, "A user's guide to the ambiguous word 'epigenetics,'" *Nature Reviews, Molecular Cell Biology*, Vol. 19, Issue 4, April 2018, 207-208, https://pubmed.ncbi.nlm.nih.gov/29339796.

3. Bruce Lipton, "The rise of the phoenix: an evolving global humanity," LivingNow, August 28, 2009, https://livingnow.com.au/rise-phoenix-evolving-global-humanity.

4. "Epigenetics & Inheritance," Learn.Genetics, accessed July 2, 2021, https://learn.genetics.utah.edu/content/epigenetics/inheritance.

5. Bob Weinhold, "Epigenetics: the science of change," *Environews: Environmental Health Perspectives*, Vol. 114, No. 3, March 1, 2006, https://doi.org/10.1289/ehp.114-a160.

6. Rachel Yehuda, et. al., "Transgenerational Effects of Posttraumatic Stress Disorder in Babies of Mothers Exposed to the World Trade Center Attacks during Pregnancy," *The Journal of Clinical Endocrinology & Metabolism*, Volume 90, Issue 7, July 1 2005, 4115–4118, https://doi.org/10.1210/jc.2005-0550.

CHAPTER FOUR

THE SCIENCE OF FEAR

There is no fear in love. But perfect love drives out fear, because fear has to do with punishment. The one who fears is not made perfect in love (1 John 4:18).

Deliverance ministry is the administration of perfect love. Jesus demonstrated this fact consistently throughout His earthly ministry as He healed the sick and cast out demons. As believers in Jesus, we are commanded not to fear so often in scripture that it is impossible to ignore. In fact, the Bible says "do not be afraid" more than 70 times. What is the appropriate response to a command such as "do not be afraid"? It is one thing to be told not to be afraid; it is quite another to actually walk out that command. Look toward the end of this book for prayers and resources that will help you walk out your freedom.

The good news is that we don't need special tools or extravagant prayers to walk a life of freedom. Our first method is given to us in Exodus 14:13: *"Do not be afraid, stand firm and you will see the deliverance the Lord will bring you today."*

Here the scripture is simple—first do not be afraid, followed by an explanation how to accomplish this task. Stand firm is an intentional position taken both in the natural and in the spirit to overcome the spirit of fear. We must engage our minds, our will, and our emotions to focus on the promises of God, which according to this scripture is deliverance from fear.

While this verse in Exodus would be enough for us to take an obedient stand for our freedom, God wanted to really lock in the message. So, we continue to read in Luke 12:22-32—do not worry, seek the kingdom, do not be afraid, your Father is pleased to give you the kingdom. Again, we have the command *do not worry or be afraid*. And again, it is followed with simple instructions to accomplish this task. *Seek the kingdom* and *stand firm* are the prescribed methods to overcoming fear in our lives, according to these verses.

To further sweeten the benefits of living a fearless life, God concludes both scriptures with a promise. In Exodus 14:13, the promise for living free of fear is that you will be delivered. And the promise in Luke 12:32 is that your Father is *"pleased to give you the kingdom."* Both are powerful promises of deliverance from oppression and torment. Beyond that, walking away from fear delivered and in possession of the kingdom is the adoption of a new identity. One that overflows with the renewed life of confidence and joy.

Both our deliverance and possession of the kingdom are contingent on our obedience in following God's command, "do not fear."

Fear Is Witchcraft

I usually make that statement as an opening when I present this teaching live. Many times I'm met with three responses. The first response is usually, "Wow, I am not sure I believe that statement; it's a bit of a stretch." The second response is usually a resounding "Yes, I agree." And the third response is a quizzical look waiting for me to provide a bit more substance before rendering judgment. Whatever position you take, I will demonstrate how fear is exactly the definition and essence of witchcraft.

Since the beginning of recorded history, humanity has demonstrated fear in some aspect. Adam and Eve were afraid in the garden after disobeying God in Genesis 3:10:

> He [Adam] *answered, "I heard you in the garden, and I was afraid because I was naked; so I hid."*

Fear is the first negative emotion mentioned in the Bible. The fact that fear is immediately present following disobedience is not a coincidence. This was the strategy of satan to introduce the spirit of fear into the world through the open door of willful disobedience. The reason fear is so powerful is that it is more than a simple emotion; fear is a tormenting spirit: *"for God gave us a spirit not of fear but of power and love and self-control"* (2 Tim. 1:7 ESV); and as such requires a spiritual solution to remove it:

> *There is no fear in love, but perfect love casts out fear. For fear has to do with punishment, and whoever fears has not been perfected in love* (1 John 4:18 ESV).

What happened in the garden between Eve, the serpent (satan), and eventually Adam was a manipulative event—fear entered the world and the manipulation of God's people became satan's greatest tool against humanity.

Earthly culture understands fear and uses it as a manipulative tool to sell merchandise and motivate people emotionally into doing things they would not ordinarily do if fear were not present. The following is a quote from a researcher summarizing a book titled *The Science of Fear: How the Culture of Fear Manipulates Your Brain* by Dan Gardner:

> A lot of what humans fear springs from how humans miscalculate risks. This constant tussle between what Gardner characterizes as "gut" (old brain) and "head" (new brain) does not always slant to the corner of reason and logic. It seems to be a lot easier to accept seditious fear than to be calmed by probability and statistics. These gut-based fears are reddened and escalated by ubiquitous societal fear mongering. Politicians use it. The media lives by it ("if it bleeds it's on page one"). Corporations and special interest groups fatten their revenue with it. It's everywhere.[1]

Fear is a tool used by the world and the enemy to manipulate and control. This is the very essence of witchcraft being demonstrated in every insurance commercial, medication commercial, and in doctors' offices throughout the world.

Fear and Anxiety Share Similarities

"Ethologists define fear as a motivational state aroused by specific stimuli that give rise to defensive behavior or escape."[2] Simply put, fear and anxiety are two sides of the same coin and are triggered by events in our lives that lead us to behave in certain unwanted ways. For example, think of that moment you pulled a letter from the mailbox and read that it was from the Internal Revenue Service. Unless you were expecting a check (unlikely), you probably experienced an unwanted reaction in your body. Anxiety and fear in the form of sweats, increased heart rate, worry, weakness, and a whole litany of "what if" questions passing through your mind. The anxiety felt in this instance is what is known as a generalized response to an *unknown* threat or internal conflict, whereas fear is focused on *known* external danger.

Now that we understand fear is a manipulative tool used by satan to subjugate and control, we can better understand how to fight it. According to the medical community, treatments for fear and anxiety are limited and pharmaceuticals have little effect in reducing or eliminating them. However, we know from the Bible that fear and anxiety is a spirit, which is why medical treatment can only bring limited relief. Spiritual healing is required for complete freedom. Spiritual treatment of fear and anxiety begins with Second Timothy 1:7, *"God has not given us a spirit of fear, but of power and of love and of a sound mind"* (NKJV). Simply put, the love of God drives out fear. Next, Philippians 4:6-7, *"Do not be anxious about anything, but in every situation, by prayer and petition, with thanksgiving, present your requests to God. And the peace of God, which transcends all understanding, will guard your hearts."*

Once again, the spiritual prescription is to pray and give your requests to God. From there He will replace the fear with peace and love.

Impacts of Fear on Our Bodies and Mind

Now that we understand fear is a form of witchcraft designed by satan to manipulate, control, and suppress the body of Christ, we will take a look at the impact of fear on our bodies and minds. Physically, our bodies cannot handle the enduring stress that fear places on them. Many studies have been conducted that show exactly how harmful fear is on our physical bodies and our ability to process cognitive thought. What follows are the results of some of these studies.

A Northwestern University study looked at the brain, specifically the amygdala, concerning its reaction to fear. The amygdala is the part of the brain responsible for emotion processing and fear response. The study revealed that when fear is present the amygdala triggers several body-impacting and life-impacting changes. First, the stress hormone cortisol is released; next comes elevated blood pressure followed by a release of norepinephrine from the adrenal gland, which is similar to adrenaline. Further, when we ruminate or worry about a problem in life, our bodies continuously release cortisol. News flash! Our bodies were not designed to operate on a constant supply of cortisol, or any fear hormone for that matter. Elevated levels of cortisol can lead to serious problems. For example, in addition to increased blood pressure, the immune system is suppressed, blood sugar begins to rise, along with a decrease in libido, increased acne, obesity, and more.[3]

As you are likely beginning to understand, the spirit of fear does not play nice. You might be thinking that the previously stated issues are pretty damaging and life-altering. And you are correct to think that; however, the issues don't stop there. As we continue to understand fear's impact on our bodies, we look also at its impact on our minds and thoughts. For example, when fear is present in our lives, our cerebral cortex actually winds down and stops working. It is important to understand that our cerebral cortex is the part of our brain that is responsible for making us, "us." Our ability to think, reason, make decisions, conduct higher thought, and even our consciousness is handled by our cerebral cortex. But in the presence of fear, these functions do not work as intended. That is because all energy is diverted to a fight-or-flight response even though you may not actually be physically running or fighting. Fear causes our minds to bypass the thinking process completely and we become responders only. The implication is that fear causes people to become blinded, susceptible, hoodwinked, and easily deceived by the enemy. This is exactly why the enemy wants to control our thoughts so badly. Demonic assignments create fear and thus reduce ability to think, and this makes for a perfect playground for the enemy. Long-held fears and phobias eventually become life incapacitating and debilitating, robbing us of our identity as children of God and rendering us unable to fulfill our God-given purposes. Yet fear was intended by God as a mechanism to keep us safe. We must have balance—if a bear is chasing you, the wisdom in that situation is to be afraid so you take action and protect yourself. But once the fear-inducing event has concluded, our bodies should resume normal operation. The negative effects of fear addressed in this chapter stem from *chronic* fear and anxiety.

The American Journal of Managed Care published a list of known effects of fear on our health. The study shows chronic fear causes our body's immune system to become compromised and vulnerable. As I write this book, the world is currently experiencing what is being called a pandemic. The virus COVID-19 has swept the earth and created an environment of fear among the entire world's population. People are afraid to be in public without wearing a mask while they wait for the promise of a vaccine. Speaking anecdotally, observing society during this time we watched as fear-laden news warned us of impending spread of the virus and advised people to stay home. Knowing what we know of the effect of fear on our immune systems, we can also see how people became more susceptible as fear of the virus compromised their immune systems and therefore made them more likely to succumb to the very thing they feared.

The American Journal of Managed Care documents that fear can also cause the entire endocrine system to malfunction. The endocrine system is responsible for mood regulation, growth, metabolism, and reproduction. Continuing the list, negative side effects of fear include:

- The autonomic nervous system is impaired.
- Sleeping disorders increase.
- Chronic fatigue sets in and wears down the body.
- Changes in the hypothalamus-pituitary-adrenal axis. (This is essentially a whole body response.)

According to the AJMC, a secular medical journal, the potential consequences of chronic fear on spiritual health are:

- Bitterness/fear toward God or others
- Confusion/disgust with God or religion
- Loss of trust in God and/or clergy
- Waiting for God to fix it
- Despair related to perceived loss of spirituality[4]

It is said that knowledge is power. We now know exactly how the enemy targets our lives using a spirit of fear. We are empowered and equipped to appropriately identify and address the intrusive and unwelcome spirit of fear. Never again allow the spirit of fear to manipulate, debilitate, or suppress your God-given rights in the kingdom as a child of God.

Overcoming Fear

How then do we fight and overcome the stronghold of fear in our lives? Once again the Bible provides the answers to this worldly and demonic problem. We fight fear with a personal relationship with God our Father. Remember, love drives out all fear (see 1 John 4:18). God did not mean for us to battle alone. As believers in Christ, we replace the lie of fear with the truth of love, encouragement, surrounding ourselves with relationships that build us up and edify and enrich our lives.

> *Let us hold unswervingly to the hope we profess, for he who promised is faithful. And let us consider how we may spur one another on toward love and good deeds, not giving up meeting together, as some are in the habit of doing, but encouraging one another—and all the more as you see the Day approaching* (Hebrews 10:23-25).

Next, seek out and submit to sound biblical deliverance of the stronghold of fear, anxiety, rejection, heaviness, and deaf-muteness, which causes mental confusion. Receive inner healing for trauma in your bloodline and in your life that is being used by the enemy to maintain his grasp. Cultivate a lifestyle where you confess spiritual truths and blessings over yourself daily. Build yourself up using the words Jesus would use to describe you. Finally, cultivate a lifestyle of forgiveness and gratitude, making them habits. We will provide you with tools to accomplish all of this in the final chapter of this book.

It is believed that consciously identifying anxious thinking is enough to reduce anxiety. How much more effective can we be when we go beyond identifying the anxiety and begin to speak and declare a complete removal of the anxiety, to be intentionally replaced with love, joy, and peace of the Holy Spirit? Fear is the virus; love is the cure. Look toward the end of this book for methods to overcome fear and anxiety. We conclude this chapter on fear with biblical truths that will shatter the enemy's grip.

> For the Spirit God gave us does not make us timid, but gives us power, love and [sound judgment] (2 Timothy 1:7).
>
> There is no fear in love. But perfect love drives out fear, because fear has to do with punishment. The one who fears is not made perfect in love (1 John 4:18).
>
> I sought the Lord, and he answered me; he delivered me from all my fears (Psalm 34:4).
>
> The Lord is my light and my salvation—whom shall I fear? The Lord is the stronghold of my life—of whom shall I be afraid? When the wicked advance against me

to devour me, it is my enemies and my foes who will stumble and fall. Though an army besiege me, my heart will not fear; though war break out against me, even then I will be confident (Psalm 27:1-3).

God is our refuge and strength, an ever-present help in trouble. Therefore we will not fear, though the earth give way and the mountains fall into the heart of the sea, though its waters roar and foam and the mountains quake with their surging. There is a river whose streams make glad the city of God, the holy place where the Most High dwells. God is within her, she will not fall; God will help her at break of day. Nations are in uproar, kingdoms fall; he lifts his voice, the earth melts. The Lord Almighty is with us; the God of Jacob is our fortress (Psalm 46:1-7).

NOTES

1. Leonard L. LaPointe, PhD, "Science of Fear," *Journal of Medical Speech-Language Pathology*, Vol. 17, Issue 2, June 2009, VII-VIII, https://www.researchgate.net/publication/298513758_Science _of_Fear.
2. Thierry Steimer, PhD, "The biology of fear- and anxiety-related behaviors," *Dialogues Clin Neurosci*, Vol. 4, Issue 3, September 2002, 231–249, https://www.ncbi.nlm.nih.gov/pmc/articles/ PMC3181681.
3. Sarah Klein, "Adrenaline, Cortisol, Norepinephrine: The Three Major Stress Hormones, Explained," HuffPost Life, Cortisol, April 19, 2013, https://www.huffpost.com/entry/adrenaline-cortisol -stress-hormones_n_3112800.

4. Jaime Rosenberg, "The Effects of Chronic Fear on a Person's Health," *The American Journal of Managed Care,* November 11, 2017, https://www.ajmc.com/view/the-effects-of-chronic-fear -on-a-persons-health.

CHAPTER FIVE

THE SCIENCE OF REJECTION

A lady we'll call Lisa was having a difficult time with her self-worth. She felt that she was unattractive, unintelligent, and that people did not want to be friends with her. As we listened to her talk, we could see none of this was true. However, because she thought it to be true, it brought very real emotional pain to her. The question was, why did her perception of herself differ so vastly from reality? In reviewing her deliverance questionnaire and interviewing her in detail, we saw that she had endured a marriage to someone who was verbally abusive, who often put her down and said those very things to her: "You are ugly," "You are stupid," and "Nobody wants you." The marriage had ended decades earlier, and Lisa felt she had "gotten over it." In her mind, it was so far in the past that it was a non-issue. What she had failed to see was that those words had wounded her; they had left a mark. And because the wound had not been addressed, it continued to affect how she felt and thought about herself. She recognized that her ex-husband had been abusive, and intellectually she knew what he said was untrue, that it was a control tactic. But what we know in our intellect and what we feel in our hearts (and thus what has been programmed into our minds and bodies) can be worlds apart. Her soul and body still carried the rejection impact of those words.

Unhealed pain of the past spurs a protective mechanism of hypervigilance. It prompts us to filter every situation through a pain filter, in attempt to detect and deflect any future occurrence of that same pain.

In Lisa's case, in her current social interactions she was blowing minor offenses out of proportion. At times she was also perceiving rejection where there wasn't any. All of this because of her protective filter. And because she was hiding behind a protective screen of sorts, she sometimes came across to others as cold and standoffish, thus causing them to retreat, and her to feel even more rejected. Through the ministry process, the Holy Spirit gently unearthed the lies she had unknowingly believed about herself. He cleansed the wound and healed it so that she could move forward without the haze of pain that kept her from seeing herself, others, and even God clearly. She learned to accept her heavenly Father's embrace and to allow Him to be her protector, instead of that old filter of pain.

Rejection is an emotional wound universally shared by all human beings. It goes back to the immediate consequences God was forced to invoke on Adam and Eve as a result of their sin in the Garden of Eden. They were evicted from the only home they had ever known, and God put a guard at the entrance to keep them out. While we know God was not in actuality rejecting them (He was already working on His incredible plan for redemption), we can still imagine how they might have felt. Being excluded, suddenly feeling distant from God, feeling the weight of sin—all of this would have fed into the feeling of rejection. Perhaps this ancient root is the reason why every person I have ministered to so far has needed healing from rejection in some way, shape, or form.

Not all cases of rejection seem as drastic as Lisa's story above. A person may have received less attention from their parents than their special-needs sibling, and even though their parent did not love them any less, the child perceived it as rejection. A person may have had a high school teacher tell them they weren't very talented and should not pursue a certain career. These things may seem less dramatic than a story of abuse or abandonment, but the pain of rejection is subjective, not proportional. It only takes a "small" wound for the enemy to get a foothold in our thought life that he can leverage and build upon for years to come. This is why we need the Holy Spirit to intervene, to reveal and heal *every* wound.

Rejection is an emotional wound, yes. But we will also examine the science that, left unchecked, it causes *physical* ailments. We will also look at some of the factors that play into rejection, such as isolation, loneliness, and depression.

Rejection Is Physically Painful

"Sticks and stones may break my bones, but words will never hurt me," or so goes the rhyme many of us learned as children. In our ministry, we often hear people try to rationalize that they are not affected by the rejection they suffered in the past, because it was just "words." They say things like, "We were just kids saying stupid things to each other; I'm old enough to know better now," or, "I just don't let other people's opinions bother me." Or they make excuses for the person saying things like, "I know that person was in a bad situation and they were lashing out." These things may be true to a degree, but the thing is, rationalizing why we "shouldn't" feel pain does not take away the pain!

While we have been conditioned to believe that only the mentally weak are hurt by words, it turns out nothing could be further from the truth! Feeling rejected due to words or actions of others elicits a pain response in the body. Brain scans have revealed that emotional pain incurred from *rejection* registers in the same region of the brain as the emotional component of *physical* pain. In other words, your brain sees very little difference between the two types of pain. A study by Edward Smith, a cognitive neuroscientist at Columbia University in New York, found that when people were asked to look at photos of their ex-romantic partners who had rejected them, the same part of the brain lit up as when those people experienced pain from a heated probe attached to their arms.[1] In fact, scientists have found that participants who take pain relievers prior to undergoing an experiment in social exclusion experience less pain from rejection.[2] This means the same drug used to inhibit physical pain also inhibits pain from rejection! (Note: Tylenol/acetaminophen is *not* a recommended treatment for the pain of rejection.)

Our experience in ministry backs this up. For instance, in cases of physical abuse, people do experience trauma and pain from bodily injuries. However, the emotional fallout, including the pain of rejection, is just as traumatic and takes much longer to heal. We can no longer afford to pretend that emotional pain is not real, that it is less important or less impactful than physical pain. We can no longer assert that admitting to emotional pain is a weakness or that we can simply "get over it" by ignoring what we feel. Rejection is a wound to the soul *and* body, a deep emotional cut that requires cleansing, stitching up, plus application of ointment and bandages, so to speak. And as we will discuss later on in the ministry chapter, this is where God's brilliant design for healing comes in!

Common Roots of Rejection

It is important to realize how rejection gets a foothold in the first place, because addressing the root cause speeds the healing process (and helps us avoid future pitfalls). Here we will look at these common roots of rejection:

1. Orphan mindset
2. Exclusion
3. Loneliness and isolation
4. Feeling not wanted or not good enough

Orphan Mindset

The first root of rejection is common to all mankind; it is the orphan mindset.

We have various friends in our lives who have undertaken the beautiful and amazing task of adopting orphaned children—some from foster care here in the US and some from orphanages internationally. They bring these precious children into their homes, where they are loved, provided for, and cared for. They bestow upon them their family name and accept them unconditionally. But if you listen to the stories these families tell, this is just the beginning of the road to healing for these children. A child who has lived as an orphan has developed *mindsets* and *behaviors* based on their *experiences*. These include fear-based protective responses born out of lack, separation, uncertainty, loneliness, and rejection. They may have also experienced the trauma of abuse and neglect. Thus, even having arrived at a haven of love and safety, they still have knee-jerk reactions based in fear and self-preservation. They still filter information and make decisions based on the paradigm of an orphan's disadvantage.

According to the Center for Cognitive-Developmental Assessment and Remediation, post-orphanage behavior may include:

Poor Self-Regulation

- Being "reactive" rather than thinking and planning
- Difficulty setting and accomplishing goals
- Emotional volatility—extreme levels of emotion that are released without modulation, and switching between emotions suddenly and frequently
- Reluctance/unwillingness to perform tasks that are repetitive, uninteresting, require effort, and that have not been chosen by the child
- Difficulty with delaying gratification and accepting "No" for an answer

Mixed Maturity

- For example, having the self-reliance and ability to perform chores of a much older child, while having the emotional reactions of a much younger child

Self-parenting

- Behaving as someone who is resigned to taking care of themselves, thus rejecting and superseding the role of their parents as caregivers. This may include:
    - Trying to prove self-worth by attempting "important" tasks they are not yet mature enough to handle
    - Inappropriately "bossing others around" including parents, siblings, teachers, etc.
    - Taking "justice" into their own hands rather than going through proper channels to resolve disputes

Learned Helplessness

- Being needy or high-maintenance to get attention; even discipline is better than being unnoticed
- Though this seems at odds with "self-parenting," both behaviors may be found in the same child

Controlling and Avoiding Behavior

- Refusing to try something perceived as difficult due to fear of failure

- Wanting to maintain control of every situation in attempt to feel secure and safe

Self-soothing and Self-stimulating Behavior

- Having endured neglect, abandonment, and deprivation, the child develops behaviors to sooth their own emotional needs, such as sucking on their fingers, twisting their hair, rocking, spinning, etc.

Hyper-vigilance and "Pro-active" Aggressiveness

- Displaying higher levels of aggressive behavior
- Living in a state of "hyper-arousal," a heightened alertness and vigilance; this skews their ability to correctly process situations, especially emotions, and this often damages their relationships with others
- Boys may behave proactively tough, aggressive, and dominant, because they continually expect a hostile environment
- Girls may behave in a seductive or promiscuous way that is inappropriate for their age in attempt to feel in control of their situation

Feeling of Entitlement

- Orphanage life means food and supplies are rationed out evenly among everyone
- Consequently, orphans are conditioned to the mindset that they are owed the same as whatever

they see their neighbor get (regardless of whether they actually need it or have earned it)

Extreme Attention Seeking

- Tailoring behaviors to provoke a reaction and gain attention above all else
- Caring more about how people react to what they are doing than the appropriateness or effectiveness of what they are doing
- The goal is not to accomplish a task, but rather to gain approval for accomplishing the task

Indiscriminate Friendliness with Strangers

- Being open and demonstrative with strangers while aloof and restrained with their own family
- Even after being adopted, always on the lookout for potentially new or better parents; always scoping out "options" in case their current family should reject them, or because maybe a new family would be able to better fill the inner void of rejection[3]

Paradigm of Lack and Competition

We added this one to the list based on the testimonies of adoptive families:

- Hoarding food or goods for fear of a future shortage

- Eating to excess, as though there may not be enough at the next meal, or eating quickly in order to get more before it's all taken
- Being jealous of someone else doing well, getting attention, or getting some coveted item, as though there is a finite amount of those things and "more for you equals less for me"

Even after the miracle of adoption has occurred, it takes time to overcome fear, learn a whole new worldview, and to subsequently change ingrained behaviors.

Why are we spending so much time talking about orphans?

Because when humankind fell due to sin, we *all* became like orphans. We were separated from our Father. And while God immediately told Adam and Eve of His plan to restore them, they still felt the pain of that separation. They still felt, shame, fear, and rejection. That was the very beginning of orphanhood, and since that time each of us have needed the miracle of being adopted into God's family. Every human since has inherited an innate sense of rejection that came as part and parcel of our sin nature.

Think about it carefully and ask the Holy Spirit:

1. What are my fear-based protective responses?
2. Are my fear responses born out of poverty, lack, separation, abandonment, uncertainty, loneliness, rejection, trauma, abuse, or neglect? Or something else?

3. What are the ways I filter information and make decisions based on the paradigm of an orphan's disadvantage?

You see, we have all displayed one or more of the orphan behaviors listed above! They may look a bit different in the life of an adult, but the basic behaviors and motivating beliefs are still the same. Let us consider different ways the *spiritual* mindset of an orphan shows up in an *adult*:

Adult Poor Self-Regulation:

- Being "reactive," rather than thinking and planning
- Difficulty setting and accomplishing goals
- Emotional volatility
- Reluctance/unwillingness to perform tasks that are repetitive, uninteresting, require effort, and that have not been chosen by the adult
- Difficulty with delaying gratification and accepting "No" for an answer

Adult Mixed Maturity

- For example, having the ability to perform the technical tasks of an adult, but having the emotional reactions of a teenager or child—temper tantrums, sulking, pouting, shutting down, etc.

Adult Self-Parenting or Extreme Self-Reliance

- Having an attitude that "I have to go it alone" because "no one else is going to take care of me"
- Taking on tasks you aren't equipped to handle while refusing to admit you aren't equipped and refusing to ask for help or training
- Inappropriately exercising authority over others
- Taking "justice" into their own hands rather than going through proper channels to resolve disputes

Adult Learned Helplessness

- Being needy or high-maintenance to get attention

Adult Controlling and Avoiding Behavior

- Refusing to try something perceived as difficult due to fear of failure
- Wanting to maintain control of every situation in attempt to feel secure and safe

Adult Self-soothing and Self-stimulating Behavior

- OCD behaviors
- Using food, alcohol, drugs, parties, exercise, sex, entertainment, or anything else as a way to cope with or escape from emotions (rather than facing them and healing them)

Adult Hyper-vigilance and "Pro-active" Aggressiveness

- Displaying higher levels of aggressive behavior

- Living in a state of "hyper-arousal," a heightened alertness and vigilance—this skews their ability to correctly process situations, especially emotions, and this often damages their relationships with others
- Men may behave proactively tough, aggressive, and dominant, because they continually expect a hostile environment
- Women may behave in a seductive or promiscuous way, in attempt to feel in control of their situation

Adult Feeling of Entitlement

- The mindset that you are owed the same as whatever you see your neighbor get (regardless of whether you actually need it or have earned it)
- Comparison, jealousy, and anger because you don't feel life is "fair"

Adult Extreme Attention Seeking

- Tailoring behaviors to provoke a reaction and gain attention above all else
- Caring more about how people react to what you are doing than the appropriateness or effectiveness of what you are doing
- The goal is not to accomplish a task but rather to gain approval for accomplishing the task

Adult Indiscriminate Friendliness with Strangers

- Being open and demonstrative with strangers while aloof and restrained with your own family
- Always on the lookout for potentially new or better people to mentor you or fill your needs—better friends, a better spouse, a better boss, a better pastor or church; flitting from one person to the next with no endurance or commitment in relationships

Paradigm of Lack and Competition

- Hoarding food or other items
- Eating to excess or eating too quickly
- Hyper-competitiveness—making sure you get in line first, get the most, get "the best one"
- Being jealous of someone else doing well, getting attention, or getting some coveted item, as though there is a finite amount of those things and "more for you equals less for me"
  - This can include jealousy over someone else getting a promotion, getting married, having a baby, or making a friend.

When we accept Jesus as Lord and Savior, we are adopted into the family of God, but it takes time for us to "unlearn" our orphan mindset. However, when we do take deliberate steps to unlearn that mindset and think like sons and daughters instead, the spirit of rejection that comes through orphanhood loses its grip on our lives!

Exclusion

The second root of rejection we will discuss is exclusion. For children, exclusion is often overt. Other children may say things like, "We don't want to play with you," or, "This is for big kids only; you are not allowed to come." As adults, exclusion can be a more subtle, passive-aggressive form of rejection. Maybe no one says anything rude to your face like, "You're not welcome here," but you find that you were deliberately left out.

Katrina was ten years old. She was going through a shy phase, and due to her parents' financial situation, she didn't have the fashion-forward clothes that were popular among her peers. Many of the girls her age just ignored her. But there was one girl who gave her confusing "off again, on again" friendship signals. This girl would beg her to come to her house for the day, or even for an overnight. But when Katrina would come, the girl would act as though she was a nuisance. This culminated one day when the person in question invited all the girls from their youth group over for the afternoon. Upon arriving, the younger and older girls split into two groups. Katrina was in the younger group, and they had just gone outside to play when the girl who was hosting said, "Why don't you go inside and hang out with the older girls? I think you'd like it better there."

Realizing she wasn't wanted, Katrina did just that. But the early-teen crowd did not appreciate a "little kid" joining them, and they were less subtle. One of them said, "Why are you here?" Then, pointing at the door she said, "Goodbye." Katrina had nowhere to go, and a couple of hours to go before her mother would be there to pick her up. She debated asking the host's mother to call her own mom to come and get her early, but she knew that would involve questions. She was not one to lie, and the truth that "no one wanted me around" was excruciating to admit. It would also have caused a lot of forced apologies and bred more resentment from the other girls. So, Katrina went into the living room and sat alone, passing the time in silence until her mother arrived.

A couple of years later, she found out through the grapevine that her "friend's" mom had forced the friend to invite her over a lot because she had noticed Katrina being treated like an outsider and wanted to rectify that. The friend had obeyed to appease her mother. But having complied with the letter of the law, she then let her true heart be known through her unkind actions. While it looked like a small thing to outsiders, it left Katrina feeling that something must be wrong with her, otherwise the other girls would not have been okay with excluding her that way.

Bruce was a straightforward kind of guy. While he generally wasn't rude, he always voiced his true opinions. On paper, his place of work claimed to value out-of-the-box thinking and those who would creatively challenge the status quo for the betterment of the company. However, this did not always hold true in practice. Certain people in management preferred to have things go "smoothly" as they rolled out new projects, and this meant having people on the project team who would generally go along with management's preferences, no questions asked. One day, Bruce found he hadn't been invited to a project meeting the previous week, one that dealt with a major transition for the department he managed. He was surprised but dismissed it as an oversight. However, as the weeks went by it continued to happen. Decisions rolled down the pipeline and were communicated to him by email—decisions on which he had not been consulted even though his high level of expertise and experience would have a great impact. When he questioned his management over his lack of involvement, they answered with vague language that did nothing to explain the situation.

While Bruce was understandably bothered by the logistical impacts to his department, he was also left feeling like he no longer had a voice and that his input was not wanted or valued. He no longer felt respected in his place of work. It left him second-guessing all his past interactions; had he been too bold, too forceful? Had he made a slip-up somewhere that lowered people's opinions of him? The exclusion he experienced left him feeling uncertain of himself and rejected.

Sometimes Exclusion Happens Unintentionally.

Emily was new in town and joined a play group so that her young children could make friends over the summer. When she arrived, the other moms seemed friendly, smiling and asking her name and the ages of her kids. But the conversation shifted very quickly, and it became apparent the other moms all attended the same church and had been friends for years. They discussed the activities their children all attended together, how the ladies' retreat had gone last week, and how they all felt about the church possibly moving to a larger building in a different part of town. Several times when conversation lulled, Emily tried to introduce new topics and to ask the other ladies about themselves. But inevitably, conversation always turned back to things common to the group of friends. Emily was unable to contribute to that exclusive sort of conversation, so she sat quietly waiting for someone to take notice of that fact and shift the topic to something more general, or perhaps even to invite her into the discussion by asking her some questions. But that never happened, and the group hardly seemed to notice or care when she said goodbye, corralled her kids, and went home. While the other moms likely had no bad intentions, their lack of awareness and consideration for someone new left her feeling like an outsider— overlooked and excluded.

Michelle was a college student, paying her own way through school and trying to make ends meet. She had a close group of friends who helped and supported each other as they made their way through each new challenge. Her friend Jenny suggested the whole group go on a trip together over spring break. They all became excited over the idea and planned to make it happen. Then Michelle's car broke down. She needed her car to commute to her job. That meant she had to get the vehicle repaired right away, and those repairs were expensive. Michelle went over her budget repeatedly, but in the end realized this unexpected financial hit would mean she could not afford the trip. She consoled herself with the thought that it was only a few days, and she could go on other trips later. What she did not expect was for her group of friends to have such an amazing experience. Over the course of that week, they had problems, adventures, surprises, and laughter that bonded them in a new way. It was the kind of thing you cannot plan for and never really expect, but that you treasure forever when it happens. Upon their return, Michelle listened to their many stories from the trip, and while she was happy for them she felt a deep sense of loss. The others had shared a bonding experience that she had missed out on, and it felt like being left behind in a way. While it was not anyone's fault, the exclusion was real.

Whatever the reason, being left out is a painful experience. We all know that instinctively, but now science is beginning to show the reality of that pain. Many researchers have conducted various studies on social exclusion using a virtual ball-tossing game called "Cyber-Ball." Participants believe they are playing the game remotely with other people (though in reality they are playing only with a computer). The game begins with a period of "fair play," in which all players toss the ball back and forth. After a time, the computer model switches and the only real player is excluded, while the other two "players" toss the ball to each other but never to him or her. During this game, participants undergo brain scans using fMRI, or "Functional Magnetic Resonance Imaging." The findings show the emotional pain of social exclusion activated brain patterns very similar to those that occur during physical pain: "providing evidence that the experience and regulation of social and physical pain share a common neuroanatomical basis."[4]

Another study looked at the brain responses to social ostracism and concluded that people are extremely quick to recognize when it is happening to them. Additionally, the study showed that some people's brains fired the ostracism patterns even during the "fair play" portion of the game. This means we can have a perception of exclusion when there is none in reality, yet it affects our brain in the same manner as if the exclusion were real. The study concluded that this is due to "individual differences in ostracism-related distress."[5]

Exclusion, whether intentional, unintentional, or just perceived:

- Puts you through the same torment as physical pain;
- Feeds the orphan mindset we learned about above;
- Causes many people to wrestle intensely with feelings of rejection;
- Causes social awkwardness that in turn breeds more rejection.

Loneliness and Isolation

The third root of rejection is loneliness, and it is also a byproduct of rejection.

> "Not only is it not much fun to feel lonely," says Ami Rokach, a psychologist and York University professor who has been studying loneliness for nearly 30 years. "It is also dangerous."[6]

> The pain of loneliness is a deeply disruptive hurt. The disruption, both physiological and behavioral, can turn an unmet need for connection into a chronic condition.[7]

Scientists have now been studying loneliness for decades, and the results all agree that it carries with it an increased risk of premature mortality. In other words, it can kill you. However, because it is not an illness in and of itself it cannot be treated with diet or herbs or prescriptions. It must be addressed in the realm of behaviors, thought patterns, and emotional healing.

There are two major categories of loneliness—transitional and chronic.

- Transitional loneliness is what we experience when we move to a new city, attend a new school, or start a new job. It generally resolves on its own as we make new friends and acquaintances.

- Chronic loneliness is a different animal. It is not resolved by social interaction. According to Rokach, "It is the type of loneliness that can lead to illness and premature death if left unaddressed," and thus the person's mental health must be addressed.[8]

Loneliness becomes an issue of serious concern only when it settles in long enough to create a persistent, self-reinforcing loop of negative thoughts, sensations, and behaviors.[9]

When we use the term *loneliness* in this chapter, we are referring to *chronic loneliness*—the kind that has become that self-reinforcing loop of negativity.

Feelings of loneliness and isolation can stem from a lack of social interaction; this is literal isolation. For whatever reason, we have little to no contact with others. Or it can be caused by a lack of *meaningful* social interaction. This is more common than literal isolation. In this scenario, we may be around people often. We may have a spouse, children, and coworkers with whom we interact every day. But with all of that, we may not feel supported or that the deep things of our hearts are understood. We may not feel valued. This is the type of loneliness that comes from a social diet of superficial contact. It is like having a diet of candy and soda. There are calories, yes. But it does not sustain you or provide what your body needs to thrive. Over time your health will suffer, and you will crave something substantial and "real."

In fact, loneliness and hunger are an apt comparison. When you lack food, your brain sends signals that prompt you to seek out nutrients. Very similarly, when deprived of social interaction, your neurons ignite chemicals that prompt you to crave it and seek it out:

> Matthews and collaborators found that dopaminergic neurons in a brain region called the dorsal raphe nucleus were activated in response to acute social isolation and triggered the motivation to search for and re-engage in social interactions.[10]

There is also "perceived loneliness." This is when we have plenty of meaningful connection, but somehow that does not penetrate our hearts. We are stuck in an emotional plateau of "feeling" lonely, without good cause. From our experience in ministry, this is usually due to lack of meaningful connection with God Himself, and due to the unresolved hurt of loneliness from our past. Our own defense mechanisms can keep others at a distance, or keep our own emotions from connecting with others, because the pain of *past* rejection has instilled a fear of *future* rejection.

Any way you look at it, loneliness is detrimental to physical health. Let us look at some of the evidence. According to researchers, loneliness can:

- Cause stress
- Cause anxiety
- Cause depression
- Increase mortality, equivalent to smoking 15 cigarettes per day
- Pose an equal danger as substance abuse, if not a greater one[11]
- Has a negative health impact comparable to:
  - High blood pressure
  - Lack of exercise
  - Obesity (this is true of the subjective feeling of being alone, not just literally being alone)
- Accelerate the aging process
- Show up in measurements of:
  - Stress hormones
  - Immune function
  - Cardiovascular function
- Undermine our ability to think clearly
- Predict the progression of Alzheimer's disease
- "One of our recent studies suggests that loneliness actually has the power to alter DNA transcription in the cells of your immune system."[12]
- Impairs our "social cognition" (the sense we make of our interactions with others). Loneliness will

distort our perception of social cues, impair our ability to regulate our own social behaviors, in turn making us socially awkward and thus perpetuating more loneliness.

Isolation can also mean a lack of physical touch. One of our friends and mentors in deliverance ministry, Dr. Bill Sudduth, used to tell us that people on the church greeting team should be sure to shake hands with every single person who enters the building. "For some people," he would say, "that is the only physical touch they will encounter in their whole week." And it turns out that he was on to something important. Not everyone goes home to a loving family, and "no touch policies" at schools and places of work may forbid physical contact in environments outside the home.

Increasingly, scientists are finding how this affects health. Appropriate physical touch:

- Can increase natural "killer cells," the frontline of the immune system;
- Is necessary for normal growth in children;
- Is necessary for normal mental development in children;
- Decreases verbal and physical aggression in children;
- Inhibits stress hormones, such as cortisol;
- Increases serotonin, the body's natural stress inhibitor and anti-pain hormone;
- Decreases "Substance P," which senses pain.

Some studies [show] that if you get hugged by your partner before a stressful condition like giving a speech or doing math problems, people do better. Performance is better if they've been hugged by a partner before the stress.[13]

Loneliness (real or perceived) and isolation (from people or from physical touch) are huge risk factors to our physical and mental health.

Feeling Not Wanted or Not Good Enough

This is the fourth common root of rejection. This can stem from many experiences, including inherited feelings of rejection via epigenetic markers (discussed more in-depth in Chapter Two). Here, we will focus on experiences unique to the person's life. This is not an exhaustive list. Feeling not wanted or not good enough can stem from:

1. Being an unplanned pregnancy about which your family was unhappy
2. Being a girl when your family wanted a boy, or vice versa
3. Trauma during the time your mother was pregnant with you
4. Trauma during your birth
5. Being separated from your mother directly after birth
6. Being given up for adoption

Note: Regarding numbers 3–6, the baby can sense fear in the mother's emotions and is very cognizant of any separation from the mother (the only home the baby has ever known up to that point). Not knowing how to interpret these circumstances and emotions, the baby may internalize them as rejection.

7. Feeling you don't meet expectations or are below average in some area, such as talent, looks, achievements, athletic skill, academics, personality, etc.

8. Feeling you are a burden to others

9. Feeling disconnected in important relationships (parents, spouses, immediate family)

10. Feeling guilt or shame over your mistakes and sins

11. Feeling guilt or shame that others have piled on you, even when you were not at fault

12. Being abused physically, sexually, or verbally (including being "bullied")

13. Being neglected or abandoned

14. Being consistently treated with a harsh, angry, frustrated, or cold manner

15. Being fired, laid off, or demoted

16. Being rejected for promotions or new positions

17. An unfaithful spouse or romantic partner

18. Divorce, broken engagement, or breakup

19. Betrayal/backstabbing

20. Any number of events that we may have misinterpreted, especially while we were babies or children

Summary

Rejection and isolation are a type of lack in a person's life. Just as God designed us to need hydration, nutrients, oxygen, and sunlight, He also designed us to need meaningful relationship. We ignore this at our peril!

> *And let us consider how we may spur one another on toward love and good deeds, not giving up meeting together, as some are in the habit of doing, but encouraging one another—and all the more as you see the Day approaching* (Hebrews 10:24-25).
>
> *Two are better than one, because they have a good return for their labor: If either of them falls down, one can help the other up. But pity anyone who falls and has no one to help them up. Also, if two lie down together, they will keep warm. But how can one keep warm alone? Though one may be overpowered, two can defend themselves. A cord of three strands is not quickly broken* (Ecclesiastes 4:9-12).

God's design is very clear. As we move through this book we will uncover ways to recognize your own roots of rejection and partner with the Holy Spirit so that He can bring healing to you!

NOTES

1. "Study illuminates the 'pain' of social rejection," University of Michigan News, March 25, 2011, https://news.umich.edu/study -illuminates-the-pain-of-social-rejection.
2. C. Nathan Dewall, at. Al, "Acetaminophen reduces social pain: behavioral and neural evidence," *Psychological Science*, Vol. 21,

Issue 7, July 2010, 931-9377, https://pubmed.ncbi.nlm.nih.gov/20548058.

3. Boris Gindis, Ph.D., "Post-Orphanage Behavior in Internationally Adopted Children," April 2012, http://www.bgcenter.com/BGPublications/OrphanageBehavior.htm.

4. Naomi I. Eisenberger, Matthew D. Lieberman, Kipling D. Williams, "Does rejection hurt? An FMRI study of social exclusion," *Science*, Vol. 302, Issue 5643, October 10, 2003, 290-292, https://pubmed.ncbi.nlm.nih.gov/14551436.

5. Michael J. Crowley, et. al., "Exclusion and micro-rejection: event-related potential response predicts mitigated distress," *Neuroreport*, Vol. 20, Issue 17, November 25, 2009, 1518–1522, https://www.ncbi.nlm.nih.gov/pmc/articles/PMC4457507.

6. Sam Juric, "The Science of Loneliness," The Walrus, March 16, 2020, https://thewalrus.ca/the-science-of-loneliness.

7. Dr. John T. Cacioppo, *Loneliness: Human Nature and the Need for Social Connection* (New York, NY: W.W. Norton and Co., Inc., 2008).

8. Juric, "The Science of Loneliness."

9. Cacioppo, *Loneliness*.

10. Robin Joy Meyers, "The Science of Loneliness and Isolation," TED Talks, June 2019, https://www.ted.com/talks/robin_joy_meyers_the_science_of_loneliness_and_isolation.

11. Juric, "The Science of Loneliness."

12. Cacioppo, *Loneliness*.

13. Jonathan Jones, "Why Physical Touch Matters for Your Well-Being," Greater Good Magazine, November 16, 2018, https://greatergood.berkeley.edu/article/item/why_physical_touch_matters_for_your_well_being.

CHAPTER SIX

NEUROSCIENCE AND YOUR THOUGHT LIFE

Importance of Thoughts

We make something that has not yet happened into a real physical thought, which in turn impacts every one of our approximately 70–100 trillion cells. This collapsing of probabilities through our choices is called the observer effect in quantum physics.[1]

The above is a quote from Dr. Caroline Leaf, a neuroscientist for over 25 years. She is also a believer and has written extensively about how teachings from the Bible show up literally in the context of neuroscience. The Bible puts it this way: *"Do not conform to the pattern of this world, but be transformed by the renewing of your mind"* (Rom. 12:2). This means your physical brain and body are changed, *transformed* by your thoughts. Here we will examine the impact of your thoughts (both positive and negative) on your physical and spiritual freedom. For the purposes of this book, a "negative thought" is any thought that does not agree with the written word of God, the Bible.

When I ministered to Anna, I asked about the deliverance questionnaire she had filled out. She had marked many thoughts that she was experiencing, including "I will never be good enough," "I am overwhelmed," and "There is no way out." Anna was going through several crises with her children and finances simultaneously. One child was lying to her and getting into trouble online; another was lashing out at others and causing problems at school. The financial stress alone was nearly enough to break her, but the added worry for her children was wreaking havoc in her thought life. "Anna," I asked her, "what do you do when you have a barrage of these types of thoughts?"

She looked confused and said, "I don't really allow myself to have them. I'm not *supposed* to have them. I just don't let myself go there. I try to think about Jesus instead."

"But you can't just ignore these thoughts," I told her. "They reveal where you are stuck! What we need to do is acknowledge them, bring them before Jesus, and allow Him to replace them with truth."

She looked at me with a distant expression and said, "I can't. I cannot allow myself to go to that place in my head." She was terrified of opening Pandora's Box, so to speak. I let it go at the time, because as a minister I can't take anyone where they are not willing or ready to go. It wasn't until over a year later that the Lord spoke directly to Anna and she had her first breakthrough. She told me, "I was suddenly able to identify how I've been thinking and feeling. And when I faced up to it, Jesus wasn't angry with me for thinking that way! He was so loving, and He helped me to understand what has been going on inside me."

This started a healing process for Anna. Her life situation did not change overnight, but she began to have hope for her future, hope for her children, hope for her finances. She was able to start changing her behaviors in conjunction with her thoughts to start making progress. Facing up to her thought life and the simple realization that the heavenly Father was not angry with her for struggling, that He was compassionate and there to help her, brought enormous freedom.

You see, when we talk about "positive thoughts" or "optimism," we are not meaning fake cheerfulness that denies the reality of a present situation or that ignores risks or drawbacks of a decision. Nor do we mean being in denial about one's own negative thoughts or emotions and trying to simply steamroll over them with positivity. God operates both in truth and love, and we must do so as well. While the scientists who authored various studies will have their own definitions, the "positive thoughts" and "optimism" we encourage in this book mean seeking out what God says (about ourselves, about others, and about Himself) and deliberately coming into agreement with that in our own thoughts. As a principle, we agree with God even when His view or His promises seem to contradict our current reality. He is never wrong!

Facts about Thoughts

Have you ever considered what a thought *is?* Have you thought about what it is made of? Because no one else can hear our thoughts and no one else can see them, it is easy to dismiss them as not being real—to think of them as vapors of consciousness that vanish without consequence.

The reality is much different. Thoughts exist as physical structures in our brains; each one has a footprint in our gray matter. Thoughts are physical things that influence and shape other physical things. Perhaps the most well-known example is the placebo effect, where a person who is given a sugar pill will have the same benefits and/or side effects as if he was given a medication, simply because he *believes* he was given the real thing. His subconscious thoughts affected the physical matter of his body just as strongly as a drug!

Our thoughts also impact our emotions, our mental health, and our overall physical health. And as we will demonstrate, they certainly impact our spiritual health as well.

Impact of Thoughts on the Brain

Thoughts both build and change neural structure. A thought is not merely energy that flashes through our brain and then dissipates; on the contrary, thoughts create the physical structure of the brain. Thoughts create new neural pathways, new connections between neurons, or reinforce existing pathways and connections. Positive thoughts create healthy neurons. Negative thoughts damage neurons. Put another way, your thoughts can literally cause brain damage! This is not just hyperbole; doctors can observe healthy versus unhealthy neurons. The unhealthy ones become dark and shriveled. This means a doctor could look inside your head and see the structure built by your thoughts and see whether your thoughts themselves have been healthy or toxic. Neurons that have been damaged by the toxicity of negative thoughts don't just look bad; they become dysfunctional, disrupting chemical messages from the brain to the body, leading to disease and pain.

Thoughts create emotions, and positive emotions enhance:

1. Creative thinking
2. Cognitive flexibility
3. Speed of processing
4. Attention span[2]
5. Growth in the prefrontal cortex
6. Control over emotions
7. Metacognition (being aware of your own thoughts)

Negative thoughts and emotions:

1. Divert energy from the prefrontal cortex
2. Impair cognition and reduce performance capacity of the brain
3. Inhibit creative thinking
4. Reduce activity in the cerebellum, which controls coordination, balance, and speed of thought[3]

The good news is even if a brain has been damaged by negative thoughts, it can be rewired! This is called neuroplasticity. The pathways of the brain can be restored, grown, corrected, and healed!

Impact of Thoughts on Mental Health

People who think positive thoughts:

1. Produce less cortisol (stress hormone)
2. Produce more serotonin (well-being hormone)
3. Have better relationships
4. Spend less time alone and more time socializing
5. Focus better mentally
6. Tend to be healthier than negative people
7. Tend to perform better and be more successful than negative people

All of which leads to more optimism, which leads to more of all the good things listed above; it's a snowball of positivity!

People who are negative thinkers are more prone to:

1. Anxiety
2. Depression
3. Sleep disorders
4. Eating disorders
5. Hostility
6. Suicidal thoughts

If you are struggling with your mental health in any regard, addressing your thought life must be part of your treatment plan! When we minister to people, we emphasize how essential this is to their spiritual freedom. Later in the book we will learn how to do this in a biblical way.

Impact of Thoughts on the Body

Your thoughts impact your cells, your DNA, and your neurotransmitters, which carry messages between your brain and the rest of your body. Thus, it is safe to say they either directly or indirectly impact every function of your body. Here we will look at just a few of the physical benefits of aligning our thoughts with God's word.

Positive thoughts reduce the risk of heart attack.[4] Johns Hopkins researcher Lisa R. Yanek conducted a study called "Effect of Positive Well-Being on Incidence of Symptomatic Coronary Artery Disease." She and her colleagues found people with a general sense of well-being (cheerful, relaxed, etc.) were about one-third less likely to have a heart attack or sudden cardiac death. This held true even for people who were considered at higher risk due to their family history. Yanek commented, "A happier temperament has an actual effect on disease and you may be healthier as a result."[5]

Positive thoughts reduce the risk of stroke.[6] A study by researchers at New York University used data from a randomized controlled trial of 552 stroke patients in four hospitals. Prior to discharge the patients were asked if they agreed with the statement, "I can protect myself from having another stroke." One year later the researchers measured the patients' blood pressure (high blood pressure is a major risk factor for stroke). They found those who agreed with the belief that they could protect themselves had a clinically significant reduction in blood pressure over those who did not agree (this was especially accurate for women). If you believe you can protect yourself from having a stroke, that belief comes true!

Positive thoughts impact the very makeup of your being. We cover this in great detail in the chapter on epigenetics, but to summarize:

1. Thoughts activate your genes and change your genetic expression.

2. Thoughts impact your DNA.

3. Positive thoughts can preserve the length of your telomeres (scientists believe telomere dysfunction may cause DNA damage and cell death).

Positive thoughts increase resistance to the common cold.[7] Bolstering the immune system is a huge benefit of positive thinking!

Impact of Thoughts on Spiritual Freedom

So far we've been looking at the physical impact of thoughts, but what about the spiritual side? Can our thoughts impact our walk with God, or even open us up to demonic torment? As a deliverance minister I tell people if you are not willing to change your beliefs, then you will not be able to maintain spiritual freedom. You may be saved and on your way to heaven when you die, but if your thought life is a mess then you will be rendered ineffective and miserable during your time here on Earth.

To lay some groundwork for reading the following scriptures, understand that the Hebrew word *leb* can be translated "heart," "mind," or "understanding," among other things. So when you see the word *heart*, know that it refers to the thinking, conscious part of a person. First, I want to challenge the mindset that God only cares about what we do and say and not so much what we think about. On the contrary, scripture contains numerous references on the importance of our thoughts.

1. **Sin and dysfunction begin in the thoughts:**

   Such a person is double-minded and unstable in all they do (James 1:8).

   Furthermore, just as they did not think it worthwhile to retain the knowledge of God, so God gave them over to a depraved mind, so that they do what ought not to be done (Romans 1:28).

   For it is from within, out of a person's heart, that evil thoughts come—sexual immorality, theft, murder, adultery, greed, malice, deceit, lewdness, envy, slander, arrogance and folly (Mark 7:21-22).

2. **Belief in God begins in the thoughts:**

   If you declare with your mouth, "Jesus is Lord," and believe in your heart that God raised him from the dead, you will be saved (Romans 10:9).

   Everything is possible for one who believes (Mark 9:23).

3. **Worship and love of God begin in the thoughts:**

   May these words of my mouth and this meditation of my heart be pleasing in your sight, Lord, my Rock and my Redeemer (Psalm 19:14).

   "Teacher, which is the greatest commandment in the Law?" Jesus replied: "Love the Lord your God with all your heart and with all your soul and with all your mind" (Matthew 22:36-37).

4.   Personal transformation, or the "working out" of our salvation, begins in the thoughts (see Phil. 2:12-13):

> *You were taught, with regard to your former way of life, to put off your old self, which is being corrupted by its deceitful desires; to be made new in the attitude of your minds; and to put on the new self, created to be like God in true righteousness and holiness* (Ephesians 4:22-24).
>
> *Therefore, I urge you, brothers and sisters, in view of God's mercy, to offer your bodies as a living sacrifice, holy and pleasing to God—this is your true and proper worship. Do not conform to the pattern of this world, but be transformed by the renewing of your mind. Then you will be able to test and approve what God's will is—his good, pleasing and perfect will* (Romans 12:1-2).

5.   We are to invite the Lord to examine our thoughts and bring change where needed:

> *Search me, God, and know my heart; test me and know my anxious thoughts. See if there is any offensive way in me, and lead me in the way everlasting* (Psalm 139:23-24).
>
> *Create in me a pure heart, O God, and renew a steadfast spirit within me* (Psalm 51:10).

It is because of this enormous importance of our thoughts that the enemy seeks to derail our thought life. Our thoughts are the small rudder that steers the entire ship. Enemy spirits cannot control our thoughts, nor can they hear them. They can, however, influence our thoughts if we allow them to do so. Our thoughts are the perfect inroad by which they can distract us, torment us, tempt us, and even lead us. This influence comes in the form of demonic whispers, and they are experts at making their words sound like our own thoughts. Thus, they will phrase them in first person, using vernacular that is in keeping with our own typical speech patterns.

1. "I hate the way I look."
2. "I've messed things up again!"
3. "That was a dumb thing to say. Those people are probably laughing behind my back."
4. "If God cares about me, then why did He allow _____ to happen?"
5. "This is just who I am. I can't change."

With enough repetition, thoughts become beliefs. Wrong beliefs lead to wrong actions and painful consequences. In ministry, we see people caught in negative cycles of failed relationships, health problems, feeling "stuck" and never able to move into God's plan for their lives, and more, all due in large part to the ungodly beliefs they hold without even realizing it. Knowing this should not make us fearful; it should stir us to seek God's plan to overcome these tactics. The Lord is more powerful than any plan of the enemy!

Next up we are going to look at some of the strategies God has given us to overcome wrong beliefs, and later in the book we will pull all of this together into steps you can use to implement these principles!

The Science of Meditation and Visualization

Meditation is a topic Christians sometimes shy away from because we associate it with the New Age movement and eastern religions. However, those iterations of meditation are a corruption of a function that was designed by God. There is a righteous and scriptural way to meditate, and it serves a purpose. First, I should establish what I mean by biblical meditation. We are not talking about sitting in silence for long periods of time, in uncomfortable positions, while trying to make the mind blank. On the contrary! We are talking about a state of focused, calm awareness. This is a natural state that is very beneficial to the brain and body. The mind is settled and gently focused on the present—not rehashing the past, nor worrying about the future. You have experienced this state yourself, even though you may not have thought of it as meditation! Athletes might call it "being in the zone." Musicians might call it "getting in the groove." Dancers or artists might call it "the creative flow." Normal, everyday activities can put us in a meditative state. Simple things such as going for a walk, knitting a blanket, shooting hoops, doodling or coloring, or playing an instrument. Activities involving repetitive movements that keep us engaged without being overly strenuous mentally are naturally meditative. When you are in a meditative state, you are not distracted by racing thoughts and a barrage of feelings. You are not striving or strained. You are engaged, yet emotionally relaxed.

Then there is also a more intentional type of meditation. When done with purpose and intent, meditation is an active type of brain training. This is what the Bible speaks of and what the enemy attempts to counterfeit. The counterfeit model seeks to empty the mind, to become susceptible and vulnerable to any demon that happens along, or even to invite specific demons into a person's body. The biblical model seeks to hone in on God's voice and feel His presence! It is like a way to adjust the radio dial so that the signal of His presence comes in more clearly. When you purposefully engage in biblical meditation, you utilize the same state of calm, focused awareness we discussed earlier. You may need some simple techniques to get into a meditative state (and we will give you tools for how to do this in a later chapter). Once there, you focus your thoughts with deliberate intention. You might spend time:

1. Allowing the Lord to speak to you and show you things.
2. Directing your thoughts toward thankfulness for His blessings.
3. Contemplating who He is and what He has done.
4. Reading and contemplating a passage of scripture.
5. Visualizing the things God has asked you to move toward in your life or to contend for.

It is this intentional meditation that the enemy has sought to counterfeit in pagan religions, to scare people away from within the realm of Christianity. Why? Because it is powerful. The enemy would not want to monopolize it if it were not a skill of great importance. I believe intentional meditation is a gateway to communicating with the spirit realm. This is not something to be feared, because we are protected when we ask the Holy Spirit to guard and lead that time. When we ask the Lord to preside, the enemy cannot interfere.

The Bible on Meditation

The Bible mentions meditation a great deal. King David took it for granted that he would meditate, and that his practice of meditation was to be something that pleased the Lord.

> *May these words of my mouth and this meditation of my heart be pleasing in your sight, Lord, my Rock and my Redeemer* (Psalm 19:14).

Repeatedly, we see deliberate meditation on scripture was considered a natural part of following God:

> *I meditate on your precepts and consider your ways* (Psalm 119:15).
>
> *Keep this Book of the Law always on your lips; meditate on it day and night, so that you may be careful to do everything written in it. Then you will be prosperous and successful* (Joshua 1:8).
>
> *Blessed is the one...whose delight is in the law of the Lord, and who meditates on his law day and night* (Psalm 1:1-2).
>
> *Oh, how I love your law! I meditate on it all day long. Your commands are always with me and make me wiser than my enemies. I have more insight than all my teachers, for I meditate on your statutes* (Psalm 119:97-99).

Finally, brothers and sisters, whatever is true, whatever is noble, whatever is right, whatever is pure, whatever is lovely, whatever is admirable—if anything is excellent or praiseworthy—think about such things (Philippians 4:8).

Meditation in the Bible was done as an act of worship, in the context of relationship with God. Meditating on God puts us in a state of supernatural peace and of trust in the Lord:

You will keep him in perfect peace, whose mind is stayed on You, because he trusts in You (Isaiah 26:3 NKJV).

I remember the days of long ago; I meditate on all your works and consider what your hands have done (Psalm 143:5).

I will remember the deeds of the Lord; yes, I will remember your miracles of long ago. I will consider all your works and meditate on all your mighty deeds (Psalm 77:11-12).

These scriptures teach us the results of meditating on God and His word are:

1. Peace
2. Blessing
3. Prosperity
4. His commands becoming instilled in our minds
5. Wisdom

Science on Meditation

The scientific community has made many exciting discoveries verifying the effects of meditation. Scientists describe meditation as an active type of brain training. They have found that meditation reduces pain, anxiety, and depression. A study out of Johns Hopkins found meditation to be equally effective at reducing these symptoms as antidepressant drugs.[8]

Meditation can also change the structure of your brain. Scientists at Harvard University found that a technique called *mindfulness-based stress reduction* increased volume in certain parts of the brain and decreased volume in other areas. The hippocampus increased in cortical thickness. This part of the brain is critically involved in memory and learning processes. The amygdala had a decrease in brain cell volume. This is the part of the brain that controls anxiety, fear, and stress. The participants' reports on how they *felt* afterward *matched* the physical findings. According to the study, "Mindfulness meditation has been reported to produce positive effects on psychological well-being that extend beyond the time the individual is formally meditating."[9]

Beyond that, meditating on *God* in particular changes the brain in very specific ways. Any type of meditation will change the brain, "But religious and spiritual contemplation changes your brain in a profoundly different way because it strengthens a unique neural circuit that specifically enhances social awareness and empathy while subduing destructive feelings and emotions."[10] How amazing that even beginning to contemplate the existence of God and who He is has a beneficial impact on the brains of human beings! The very act of seeking God brings health to us.

Meditation can help overcome addiction. Researchers from Yale University compared mindfulness meditation with the "Freedom from Smoking" program utilized by the American Lung Association.[11] This study found people who practiced mindfulness meditation were *much more likely* to quit smoking than those who went through the conventional program. This still held true when they conducted a follow-up 17 weeks after the study concluded.

Meditation changes our DNA. Dr. Linda E. Carlson studied breast cancer patients and found those who practiced intentional meditation preserved the length of their telomeres.[12] As explained in *Scientific American*: "Telomeres are stretches of DNA that cap our chromosomes and help prevent chromosomal deterioration—biology professors often liken them to the plastic tips on shoelaces. Shortened telomeres aren't known to cause a specific disease per se, but they do wither with age and are shorter in people with cancer, diabetes, heart disease and high stress levels. We want our telomeres intact."[13]

Visualization is a powerful component of meditation. To visualize something is simply to imagine it. God gave us the power to imagine because it is step one in the creative process. Visualization is not simply a precursor to an action, it *is* an action. It is activity and physical change in the realm of our neural network. When we visualize ourselves engaging in an activity, the same parts of the brain are activated as though we had physically engaged. Jesus Himself talked about this principle when He said: *"But I say to you that everyone who looks at a woman with **lustful intent** has **already committed adultery** with her in his heart"* (Matt. 5:28 ESV). The brain can engage in the *internal action* of adultery even when the body refrains from the *outward action*. The internal action is still an action and as such is just as "real." Thus, the sin has been committed. This applies to every type of sin, not just adultery.

On the flip side, visualization can be used for God's purposes (this was the original intent). We can become better at any action simply by imagining ourselves doing it well! In one study, researchers found that participants were able to increase muscle strength simply by visualizing themselves doing exercises.[14] In another study by Harvard University, scientists had one group of people learn to play a sequence of notes on the piano, while another group merely visualized themselves playing the same sequence. They found the brain development in the region connected with finger movements to be virtually the same.[15] This is why professional athletes are often taught to visualize themselves performing well in their sport. Visualization also conditions us to follow through with physical action. Scripture puts it this way: *"For as he thinks in his heart, so is he"* (Prov. 23:7 NKJV). Begin to imagine yourself reacting in love in tough situations. Imagine your body healing, becoming stronger and healthier. Imagine yourself doing well at the tasks to which God has called you. This is how you partner with the Lord to condition your mind for His purposes!

The Science of Affirmation: The Bible's Take

As believers in Jesus, most of us understand the importance of building each other up. But did you know that you can (and should) build yourself up as well? Romans 12:2 says to be *transformed* by the renewing of your mind. The word *mind* here means "comprehension, reason, and understanding" (Strong's #G3563). The *very next* verse (verse 3) applies to self-affirmation:

> *Do not think of yourself more highly than you ought, but rather think of yourself with sober judgment, in accordance with the faith God has distributed to each of you* (Romans 12:3).

This verse is sometimes twisted to suggest that self-deprecation equals humbleness. But read it again! It does not say to think lowly of yourself. It says "Do not think of yourself *more* highly than you *ought*." The instruction here is to think of yourself highly, but in the correct measure. You are also to think of yourself *"with sober judgment, in accordance with the faith God has distributed to each of you."* The word *soberly* here "stands before nouns designating an open place, a hollow thing, or one in which an object can be hidden" (Strong's #G1519). There is a place, or a headspace if you will, that we can enter into in order to find that which is hidden inside of us. While we are there in that headspace, we allow God to show us who we really are, and by faith we begin to agree with His assertions. When He shows us areas of sin, we repent and exercise faith that we can partner with Him in obedience and allow Him to change us. When He shows us things that are positive, we exercise faith to believe it is really true! We put aside the wrong beliefs we have about ourselves.

Left to our own devices, humans tend to lean toward extremes of either self-deprecation or haughtiness, both of which are skewed. When we allow God to show us the truth and we come into agreement with Him, our mind is renewed and we are transformed! We do this by deliberately thinking and speaking out what He shows us. We affirm ourselves with His words so that we can be transformed for His glory! When we become good at doing this, it will also change how we think about others and enable us to affirm them according to God's word for them as well.

Scientific Discoveries about Affirmation

But what about the science of affirmations? Is there any physical and mental benefit, or are we just saying nice things? In fact, research has concluded through the use of functional magnetic resonance imaging that "participants who were affirmed showed increased activity in key regions of the brain's self-processing and valuation systems when reflecting on future-oriented core values." In other words, affirmation activates the reward centers of your brain giving you an added boost mentally, spiritually, and physically, but also a better outlook on life and the possibility for a better future.[16]

Affirmation is known to take advantage of our reward circuits, This has been shown to:

1. Dampen pain
2. Maintain mental balance
3. Build a literal buffer against, pain, negativity, and threats (such as threats to self-confidence, self-efficacy, and self-concept)

Affirmation was actually designed as a protection mechanism. But how many of us actually use that mechanism? Benefits of affirmation are strongest when thinking about the future and what is possible. It is less beneficial when thinking about the past.

Affirmation requires long-term application to be beneficial.[17] Oxford University found neural pathways are increased when people practice self-affirmation tasks.[18] Specifically, the increase is in the ventromedial prefrontal cortex; this is where decisions are made. This means that having a low volume of self-affirmation lowers decision-making ability! Which we might expect to bring about more negative thinking about oneself, thus causing a snowball effect.

However, when we *do* practice self-affirmation the prefrontal cortex becomes more active! This decreases health deteriorating stress.

Biblical Affirmation

Affirmation, as we have demonstrated, is an important tool to renew our own minds. The Bible also directs us to use affirmation in ministry to others.

> *Each of us should please our neighbors for their good, to build them up* (Romans 15:2).
>
> *Therefore encourage one another and build each other up, just as in fact you are doing* (1 Thessalonians 5:11).

The question is, how do we exercise affirmation in a biblical way? The key here is to see people the way God sees them and say what He says about them! To see yourself as God sees you and say what He says about you! Speak kingdom identity over yourself and others:

1. We are friends of God.
2. We are chosen by God.

3. We are appointed by God.

4. We are bearing fruit for God (see John 15:15-17).

5. We are God's handiwork.

6. We are created to do good works—which He prepared in advance for us to do (see Eph. 2:10)!

7. We have the mind of Christ (see 1 Cor. 2:14-16).

It takes time to displace old beliefs, old thought patterns, with new ones. We'll give you more tools later on in the book, but in this moment close your eyes and ask the Lord to pinpoint one thing, one thought of yours, that needs to be adjusted.

Allow Him to show you the lie you have believed and allow Him to give you the truth to unseat it. You are on your way to having an entirely new mind!

NOTES

1. Dr. Caroline Leaf, *Think and Eat Yourself Smart: A Neuroscientific Approach* (Grand Rapids, MI: Baker Books, 2016).

2. Daniel Goleman, *Focus: The Hidden Driver of Excellence* (New York, NY: Bloomsbury, 2013).

3. Peter Mariën and Mario Manto, eds., *The Linguistic Cerebellum* (London: Elsevier Inc., 2016).

4. Lisa R. Yanek, et. al., "Effect of Positive Well-Being on Incidence of Symptomatic Coronary Artery Disease," *The American Journal of Cardiology*, Vol. 112, Issue 8, October 15, 2013, https://www.ajconline.org/article/S0002-9149(13)01280-0/fulltext.

5. Stephanie Desmon, "Don't worry, be healthy," October 1, 2013, Johns Hopkins Medicine, https://www.hopkinsmedicine.org/news/publications/hopkins_medicine_magazine/archives/fall_2013/dont_worry_be_healthy.

6. Emily Goldmann, "Positive Health Beliefs and Blood Pressure Reduction in the DESERVE Study," *Journal of the American Heart Association* Vol. 9, Issue 9, May 5, 2020, https://www.ahajournals .org/doi/10.1161/JAHA.119.014782; Rachel Harrison, "Positive Health Beliefs May Reduce Blood Pressure Post-Stroke, Especially Among Women," NYU, May 5, 2020, https://www.nyu.edu/ about/news-publications/news/2020/may/positive-health -beliefs-may-reduce-blood-pressure-post-stroke.html.

7. Mayo Clinic Staff, "Positive thinking: Stop negative self-talk to reduce stress," Mayo Clinic, accessed June 24, 2021, https://www .mayoclinic.org/healthy-lifestyle/stress-management/in-depth/ positive-thinking/art-20043950.

8. Madhav Goyal, et. al., "Meditation Programs for Psychological Stress and Well-being: A Systematic Review and Meta-analysis," *JAMA Internal Medicine*, Vol. 174, Issue 3, March 2014, 357–368, https://jamanetwork.com/journals/jamainternalmedicine/ fullarticle/1809754.

9. Britta K. Hölzel, et. al., "Mindfulness practice leads to increases in regional brain gray matter density," *Psychiatry Research*; Vol. 191, Issue 1, January 30, 2011, 36–43, https://www.ncbi.nlm.nih.gov/ pmc/articles/PMC3004979.

10. Dr. Andrew Newberg, Mark Robert Waldman, *How God Changes Your Brain* (New York, NY: Random House, 2009), 14.

11. Judson A. Brewer, et. al., "Mindfulness training for smoking cessation: results from a randomized controlled trial," *Drug and Alcohol Dependence*, Vol. 119, Issue 1-2, December 1, 2011, 72–80, https://pubmed.ncbi.nlm.nih.gov/21723049.

12. Linda E. Carlson, et. al., "Mindfulness-based cancer recovery and supportive-expressive therapy maintain telomere length relative to controls in distressed breast cancer survivors," *Cancer*, Vol. 121, Issue 3, February 1, 2015, 476–484, https://pubmed.ncbi.nlm.nih .gov/25367403.

13. Bret Stetka, "Changing Our DNA through Mind Control?" *Scientific American*, December 16, 2014, https://www .scientificamerican.com/article/changing-our-dna-through-mind -control.

14. Vinoth K. Ranganathan, et. al., "From mental power to muscle power—gaining strength by using the mind," *Neuropsychologia*, Vol. 42, Issue 7, 2004, 944–956, https://pubmed.ncbi.nlm.nih .gov/14998709.

15. A Pascual-Leone, et. al., "Modulation of muscle responses evoked by transcranial magnetic stimulation during the acquisition of new fine motor skills," *Journal of Neurophysiology,* Vol. 74, Issue 3, September 1995, 1037–1045, https://pubmed.ncbi.nlm.nih .gov/7500130.

16. Christopher N. Cascio, et. al., "Self-affirmation activates brain systems associated with self-related processing and reward and is reinforced by future orientation," *Social Cognitive and Affective Neuroscience*, Vol. 11, Issue 4, April 2016, 621-629, https:// pubmed.ncbi.nlm.nih.gov/26541373.

17. Catherine Moore, "Positive Daily Affirmations: Is There Science Behind It?" PositivePsychology.com, March 16, 2021, https:// positivepsychology.com/daily-affirmations.

18. Lesley K. Fellows and Martha J. Farah, "Role of Ventromedial Prefrontal Cortex in Decision Making: Judgment under Uncertainty or Judgment Per Se?" *Cerebral Cortex*, Vol. 17, Issue 11, November 2007, 2669–2674, https://pubmed.ncbi.nlm.nih .gov/17259643.

Chapter Seven

Gut, Brain, and Heart

A demonized person is someone who has an evil spirit attached to some part of their physical body. When we are ministering deliverance, those on our teams with a seeing gift are often able to see where the spirit is attached. Very often, we see them attached to the person's brain, heart, or gut. I have seen a client's stomach area physically move independently from the rest of their body, as though there was a boiling cauldron under their skin. This was a sudden onset reaction when we commanded the demon to come out, and it ceased as soon as the spirit left.

Although demons can (and do) attach anywhere, I have to believe there is a strategy behind it. This may be partly due to the sin inroad that allowed that spirit to attach in the first place. (Spirits can attach due to our own sin, our ancestral sin, or the wounds we have sustained because someone else sinned against us, such as trauma.) It may also be partly because they attach where they think they can leverage the most control over that particular person's life. Personally, I believe it is a combination of both. So why do we so often see them attach to the brain, gut, and heart?

It is easy to understand why a spirit would attach to a person's brain. After all, we studied the brain earlier in this book and we know how easy it might be to keep a person captive through painful unhealed memories, dysfunctional thoughts, and the resulting physical problems. With the brain being such an obvious target, why then then would a spirit attach to a different part of the body? Because the brain is not the only organ in the human body that stores memories and emotions! It is not the sole regulator of health and function.

The Gut-Brain Connection

Take for instance, the enteric nervous system. The enteric nervous system (ENS) is an arrangement of neurons and supporting cells throughout the gastrointestinal tract. It starts in the esophagus and continues to the end of the digestive tract. Did you catch that? You have neurons. In your *gut*.

> The enteric nervous system (ENS), which is sometimes considered part of the autonomic nervous system, functions largely independently to control digestion. The ENS is sometimes called the "second brain" because it contains such a diversity of neuron types, profusion of glial cells, and complex, integrated neural circuits. It's estimated 200–500 million neurons is roughly equal to the number in the spinal cord.[1]

The ENS doesn't function in the same way as the brain in your head, but still it has a reputation as the "second brain."

> The enteric nervous system doesn't seem capable of thought as we know it, but it communicates back and forth with our big brain—with profound results.[2]

Dr. Pankaj Jay Pasricha is the director for the Johns Hopkins Center for Neurogastroenterology. His research on the gut-brain connection has led to important discoveries. One of his studies concluded:

> Vagal activity, partially driven by gastric mast cells, induces long-lasting changes in Crh signaling in the amygdala that may be responsible for enhanced pain and enhanced anxiety- and depression-like behaviors. Together, these results support a "bottom-up" pathway involving the gut-brain axis in the pathogenesis of both gastric pain and psychiatric comorbidity in FD [Functional Dyspepsia].[3]

Translation: whereas depression and anxiety are known to cause digestive disease, there is evidence that the reverse can also be true—disruption in the gut can cause anxiety and depression.

The gut has direct neural connections to the brain. This is called the gut-brain axis, and communication between the brain and the gut is a two-way street via the vagus nerve. We know about this connection instinctively when we talk about having "a gut feeling," where we can't explain logically with our brain why we feel something is good or bad, but we still have a certainty about it. That is "the second brain" kicking in, or the gut communicating to the brain.

This is all well and good when the gut is healthy, but what about when it is not? There is at least one study that indicates the gut microbiome can significantly impact personality. To the point where, in mice, altering their microbiome altered their personalities and behaviors. The same study concluded that "Four-week intake of an FMPP [fermented milk product with probiotic] by healthy women affected activity of brain regions that control central processing of emotion and sensation."[4] What scientists are saying here is that the microbiome is massively important to gut health, and the gut is massively important in contributing to how we think, feel, and behave.

A person experiencing chronic emotional distress may have a gut disorder in addition to, or even instead of, a mental disorder. Doctor Pasricha went as far as to say:

> "Our two brains 'talk' to each other, so therapies that help one may help the other," Pasricha says. "In a way, gastroenterologists (doctors who specialize in digestive conditions) are like counselors looking for ways to soothe the second brain."
>
> Gastroenterologists may prescribe certain antidepressants for IBS, for example—not because they think the problem is all in a patient's head, but because these medications calm symptoms in some cases by acting on nerve cells in the gut, Pasricha explains. "Psychological interventions like CBT may also help

to 'improve communications' between the big brain and the brain in our gut," he says.[5]

And that is to say nothing of the physical issues throughout the body that can be caused by an unhealthy gut. According to an article published by the University of Washington:

> Shifts in the composition or function of the micro-biome have been implicated in inflammatory bowel disease, autism, and blood cancers. Researchers are now discovering that a disrupted microbiome, in certain contexts, may contribute to Alzheimer's disease and related conditions that cause dementia.[6]

There can be many reasons for gut imbalance, and certainly many of them are physical, such as diet. But as we have seen, physical and spiritual issues can sometime be intertwined. When a person is doing all the right things physically and still having gut issues, it is time to consider the spiritual component.

I believe one reason demons like to attach to the gut is because they can fly under the radar, so to speak. The person will be tormented by feeling "off," anxious, depressed, unsettled, and not understand why. This is because the distress signals are coming from the second brain, rather than the thinking and processing brain. The person may begin to feel something is permanently wrong with them, and helpless to get to the bottom of it. Those feelings of helplessness can lead to more depression. All of this makes the gut an easy target for demonic attachment. Thankfully, we have the authority through Jesus to break off every such attachment!

The Heart-Brain Connection

We have established that you have a brain in your head and a second brain in your gut. Now let us consider yet a third "brain" in your heart.

Professor David Paterson, Ph.D. at Oxford University, leads a research team in the area of cardiac neurobiology. He says the heart contains neurons and in his studies has called this "the heart's little brain." (The term "heart brain" was initially introduced by neurocardiologist Dr. J. Andrew Armour in 1991.) Professor Paterson asserts that the brains in the head and heart are connected because the neurons in both places fire in conjunction with each other. He has conducted experiments on neurons found on the heart's right ventricle.

> In an experiment, a piece of right ventricle from a rabbit, where these specialized neurons have been found, is placed in a tank with oxygen and nutrients. The piece of heart manages to beat on its own, despite being unattached, suspended and having no blood flowing through it. When Professor Paterson shocks the heart tissue it immediately slows down this beating. Professor Paterson believes that is a direct decision made by the neurons as they respond to the impulse.[7]

This indicates that the heart can "think" on its own, at least to a degree, apart from the signals it receives from the brain. In fact, studies have demonstrated that the heart can initiate contact with the brain and that there are four separate lines of communication:

- Neurological communication (nervous system)

- Biochemical communication (hormones)
- Biophysical communication (pulse wave)
- Energetic communication (electromagnetic fields)[8]

This may feel like a revelatory discovery of modern science, but the truth is that Bible passages written thousands of years ago have repeatedly stated that the heart can think. As we learned earlier, the Hebrew word *leb* (pronounced "labe," Strong's #H3820) can be translated "heart," "mind," or "understanding." Thus, we see scriptures that refer to the heart as "thinking," such as these:

> *Then the Lord saw that the wickedness of man was great on the earth, and that every intent of the thoughts of his heart was only evil continually* (Genesis 6:5 NASB).
>
> *For as he thinks in his heart, so is he* (Proverbs 23:7 AMP).

Just as the Bible has always indicated, it turns out the heart has many crucial functions aside from the one it is best known for—pumping our life blood. According to the HeartMath Institute:

> The heart sends us emotional and intuitive signals to help govern our lives.
>
> The heart directs and aligns many systems in the body so that they can function in harmony with one another.
>
> The heart is in constant communication with the brain. The heart's intrinsic brain and nervous system relay information back to the brain in the cranium,

creating a two-way communication system between heart and brain.

The heart makes many of its own decisions.

The heart starts beating in the unborn fetus before the brain has been formed, a process scientists call autorhythmic.

Humans form an emotional brain long before a rational one, and a beating heart before either.[9]

The institute also asserts that the heart (not the brain) is the true seat of emotional intelligence:

"Researchers began showing in the 1980s and '90s that success in life depended more on an individual's ability to effectively manage emotions than on the intellectual ability of the brain in the head," says The HeartMath Solution, by HeartMath founder Doc Childre and his associate and longtime HeartMath spokesman Howard Martin.[10]

Additionally, the heart is directly impacted by emotions:

Early HeartMath research found that negative emotions threw the nervous system out of balance and when that happened heart rhythms became disordered and appeared jagged on a heart monitor. This placed stress on the physical heart and other organs and threatened serious health problems.

"Positive emotions, by contrast, were found to increase order and balance in the nervous system and produce smooth, harmonious heart rhythms," Childre and Martin wrote. "But these harmonious and coherent rhythms did more than reduce stress: They actually enhanced people's ability to clearly perceive the world around them."[11]

We have known this intuitively when we refer to "heartbreak." All of us have felt emotional pain in our hearts at some point. We know it is real and just as painful as a physical wound. We have felt other emotions in our hearts as well, such as joy or apprehension. On some level, humans have always known that the heart is involved in perceiving and processing emotion.

But it turns out the term "heartbreak" is more literal than we may have thought. One study found that the day after losing a loved one, a person is up to 21 times more likely to die of a heart attack.[12]

In addition to its abilities to think independently and to contribute emotional intelligence to the brain, there is evidence to support the heart storing its own memories. The late Dr. Paul Pearsall was a licensed clinical neuropsychologist, clinical professor at the University of Hawaii, and a member of the heart transplant study team at the University of Arizona School of Medicine. In his book *The Heart's Code*, Dr. Pearsall shared the results of some of the interviews he conducted with 73 heart transplant patients and their families. His findings were that some heart transplant recipients took on characteristics, personality traits, and even very specific memories of their donors. These changes were confirmed by their families, and in some instances the memories were found to be quite specific to the manner of death of the donor, despite the donor's identity and personal details being undisclosed to the recipient. Some scientists theorize this may be due to cellular memory, of which there are four types: epigenetic memory, DNA memory, RNA memory, and protein memory.[13] While the theory of cellular memory transferring with the heart into the recipient is unproven, it is intriguing.

The Bible does indicate that the heart has memory when it says:

> *I have hidden your word in my heart that I might not sin against you* (Psalm 119:11).

And:

> *These commandments that I give you today are to be on your hearts* (Deuteronomy 6:6).

It becomes easy to see why demonic spirits would choose to attach to a person's heart. If they can disrupt emotional intelligence and the crucial perspective on the world around us that is normally communicated from the heart to the brain, they can render a person ineffective in following God's call on their life. If an evil spirit can keep a person in a state of chronic "brokenheartedness," never allowing memories and emotional wounds to heal, then the person remains in torment and even at risk of early demise.

The Bible on Heart Matters

Scripture has much to say about the heart.

To begin with, sin has corrupted the heart of man:

> The heart is deceitful above all things and beyond cure. Who can understand it? "I the Lord search the heart and examine the mind, to reward each person according to their conduct, according to what their deeds deserve" (Jeremiah 17:9-10).

God is the only one who can make our hearts righteous again:

> Create in me a pure heart, O God, and renew a steadfast spirit within me (Psalm 51:10).
>
> I will give you a new heart and put a new spirit in you; I will remove from you your heart of stone and give you a heart of flesh (Ezekiel 36:26).

God is the only one who can accurately know what is in a person's heart:

> The Lord does not look at the things people look at. People look at the outward appearance, but the Lord looks at the heart (1 Samuel 16:7).

We are to use our hearts to trust God:

> Trust in the Lord with all your heart and lean not on your own understanding; in all your ways submit to him, and he will make your paths straight (Proverbs 3:5-6).

We are to use our hearts to love God:

> Jesus replied: "Love the Lord your God with all your heart and with all your soul and with all your mind" (Matthew 22:37).

Desires reside in the heart:

Take delight in the Lord, and he will give you the desires of your heart (Psalm 37:4).

Wisdom resides in the heart:

The wise in heart accept commands, but a chattering fool comes to ruin (Proverbs 10:8).

Teach us to number our days, that we may gain a heart of wisdom (Psalm 90:12).

My son, if your heart is wise, then my heart will be glad indeed (Proverbs 23:15).

Doubt and belief both come from the heart:

Truly I tell you, if anyone says to this mountain, "Go, throw yourself into the sea," and does not doubt in their heart but believes that what they say will happen, it will be done for them (Mark 11:23).

See to it, brothers and sisters, that none of you has a sinful, unbelieving heart that turns away from the living God (Hebrews 3:12).

Anxiety impacts the heart:

Anxiety weighs down the heart, but a kind word cheers it up (Proverbs 12:25).

So then, banish anxiety from your heart and cast off the troubles of your body, for youth and vigor are meaningless (Ecclesiastes 11:10).

Repentance comes from the heart:

> *"Even now," declares the Lord, "return to me with all your heart, with fasting and weeping and mourning"* (Joel 2:12).

Thankfulness comes from the heart:

> *I will give thanks to you, Lord, with all my heart; I will tell of all your wonderful deeds* (Psalm 9:1).

Courage comes from the heart:

> *Though an army besiege me, my heart will not fear; though war break out against me, even then I will be confident* (Psalm 27:3).

> *Be strong and take heart, all you who hope in the Lord* (Psalm 31:24).

There is so much more I could write about the heart based on scripture alone! Seeing these passages, the Bible seems to support the scientific theory that the heart is the seat of emotional intelligence. It is also where we carry our emotional wounds.

A Testimony of Healing

When I (Petra) lost my mother, I was carrying both grief from the loss and trauma from watching her struggle with debilitating cancer.

After her death, I allowed myself to grieve and to process my questions with the Lord. In the coming year I went through some deliverance and quite a lot of inner healing. I dealt with lies I had believed, demonic attachments to the trauma, and soul ties with my mother.

All of this was beneficial, but I still felt a heaviness on my heart. It was like a tangible weight. I felt almost as though my heart had slowly frozen over and could not feel anything except for occasional sharp pangs of grief.

One night I decided on a whim (or so I thought) to go to a women's group. My intention was to sneak in a bit late, sit in the back, worship, and just feel the presence of Jesus.

God had other ideas. It was like He put a homing beacon on me and all the prophetic people in the room picked up the signal and honed in. Not long into the worship set, a woman approached me with a prophetic word. She could see the heaviness, and spoke words of hope, strength, and life that God had given her to share. She spoke over me that I was strong in the Spirit, a force to be reckoned with, which was a direct affront to the weakness and helplessness I had felt for many months. Those declarations startled me into a different mindset than when I had set foot in the door.

After I thanked her and went back to worshiping, I had a sudden sense of the veil between heaven and earth and of my mom singing worship songs to the Lord along with me, just on the other side of that veil. This was a powerful encounter, a new and very real perspective that brought great comfort.

When the meeting let out, I was approached again, this time by a trusted friend named Carolyn who was also a deliverance minister. Carolyn saw the heaviness and said, "It's like there is a shroud of grief over your heart." She prayed for the shroud to be lifted and, suddenly, it was! I felt trauma being displaced and healing come to my heart. I will always miss my mom, but I no longer carry the searing pain of the traumatic experiences.

This is what happens when God heals the heart. He knows exactly when and how to do it. It may take deliverance, a prophetic word, a gentle prayer inviting healing, a vision from heaven's perspective, or even a hug from a friend. You cannot fake or manufacture healing; just follow the Holy Spirit's lead. No matter how He does it, know that the thoughts, memories, and emotions of the heart *can* be healed. We can be free from demonic torment, free from trauma, free from heartbreak! And our heavenly Father will gently work in us until that freedom becomes our reality.

Notes

1. Bryan Kolb, *The Neurobiology of Brain and Behavioral Development*, "Chapter 3: Overview of Factors Influencing Brain Development" (London: Academic Press, 2018), 51–79.
2. Jay Pasricha, qtd. in "The Brain-Gut Connection," Johns Hopkins Medicine, accessed June 25, 2021, https://www.hopkinsmedicine.org/health/wellness-and-prevention/the-brain-gut-connection.
3. Zachary A. Cordner, et. al., "Vagal gut-brain signaling mediates amygdaloid plasticity, affect, and pain in a functional dyspepsia model," *JCI Insight*, Vol. 6, Issue 6, March 22, 2021, https://pubmed.ncbi.nlm.nih.gov/33591956.
4. Kirsten Tillisch, et. al., "Consumption of fermented milk product with probiotic modulates brain activity," *Gastroenterology*, Vol. 144, Issue 7, June 2013, 1394–1401, https://pubmed.ncbi.nlm.nih.gov/23474283.
5. Pasricha, "The Brain-Gut Connection."
6. Genevieve Wanucha, "The Gut Microbiome and Brain Health," Memory and Brain Wellness Center, October 4, 2018, http://depts

.washington.edu/mbwc/news/article/the-gut-microbiome-and
-brain-health.

7. Janey Davies, "The Human Heart Has a Mind of Its Own, Scientists
Find," Learning Mind, September 16, 2016, https://www.learning
-mind.com/the-human-heart-mind.

8. HeartMath Institute, *Science of the Heart*, "Chapter 01: Heart-Brain
Communication," accessed June 25, 2021, https://www.heartmath
.org/research/science-of-the-heart/heart-brain-communication.

9. "Heart Intelligence," HeartMath Institute, August 7, 2012, https://
www.heartmath.org/articles-of-the-heart/the-math-of-heartmath/
heart-intelligence.

10. Ibid.

11. Ibid.

12. Murray A. Mittlema, and Elizabeth Mostofsky, "Physical,
Psychological and Chemical Triggers of Acute Cardiovascular
Events: Preventive Strategies," *Circulation*, Vol. 124, Issue 3, July
19, 2011, 346–354, https://www.ncbi.nlm.nih.gov/pmc/articles/
PMC3139921.

13. Mitchell B. Liester, "Personality changes following heart
transplantation: The role of cellular memory," *Medical Hypotheses*,
Vol. 135, February 2020, https://pubmed.ncbi.nlm.nih.
gov/31739081.

CHAPTER EIGHT

THE SCIENCE OF FORGIVENESS

"To forgive is to set a prisoner free...
only to discover the prisoner was you."
—LEWIS SMEDES, Professor, Fuller Theological Seminary

Growing up in the church, forgiveness was widely taught. We are generally taught that Jesus forgave us our sins and that we should forgive others as God forgave us (see Eph. 4:31-32). It is also quite common in our culture to see parents raising children, teaching them to forgive when someone hurts them. As a body of Christ we have made forgiveness a staple of our Christian walk, and rightly so. This chapter will describe how forgiveness is the foundation of healing. Not just mentally, but physically and spiritually as well. A lot of research has been conducted over the last couple of decades by many reputable, secular, academic institutions. The results of the research may surprise you, but when we look at the research through the lens of the Bible the results are fascinating and faith building.

> *Do not seek revenge or bear a grudge against anyone among your people, but love your neighbor as yourself. I am the Lord* (Leviticus 19:18).

Scripture establishes forgiveness as a command of God in many instances. The reference above is perhaps the most poignant as it relates to the directive. God is not simply providing an optional life principle. He is telling the people here that under no circumstances are you to hold hatred or malice in your heart toward anyone. He is saying, instead, you must all find a way to love each other unconditionally. Then God takes the instruction a step further and places the capstone on the statement when He says, "I am the Lord." That's like a father of children saying "because I said so." There is no room to question the intent of the directive. The instructions are clear and no further debate is needed. Beyond the directive provided in Leviticus, the principle of forgiveness continues throughout the Bible as a theme appearing more than 152 times.

Further evidence of the validity of forgiveness in our lives is shown by Jesus when He tells the parable of the unmerciful servant.

> *Then Peter came to Jesus and asked, "Lord, how many times shall I forgive my brother or sister who sins against me? Up to seven times?" Jesus answered, "I tell you, not seven times, but seventy-seven times. Therefore, the kingdom of heaven is like a king who wanted to settle accounts with his servants. As he began the settlement, a man who*

owed him ten thousand bags of gold was brought to him. Since he was not able to pay, the master ordered that he and his wife and his children and all that he had be sold to repay the debt. At this the servant fell on his knees before him. 'Be patient with me,' he begged, 'and I will pay back everything.' The servant's master took pity on him, canceled the debt and let him go. But when that servant went out, he found one of his fellow servants who owed him a hundred silver coins. He grabbed him and began to choke him. 'Pay back what you owe me!' he demanded. His fellow servant fell to his knees and begged him, 'Be patient with me, and I will pay it back.' But he refused. Instead, he went off and had the man thrown into prison until he could pay the debt. When the other servants saw what had happened, they were outraged and went and told their master everything that had happened. Then the master called the servant in. 'You wicked servant,' he said, 'I canceled all that debt of yours because you begged me to. Shouldn't you have had mercy on your fellow servant just as I had on you?' In anger his master handed him over to the jailers to be tortured, until he should pay back all he owed. This is how my heavenly Father will treat each of you unless you forgive your brother or sister from your heart" (Matthew 18:21–35).

Peter thought he would be clever when he offered to forgive as many as seven times. The story not only taught Peter a lesson on the breadth and depth of forgiveness, but Jesus also established principles here as well. The first principle demonstrated is that forgiveness should be offered infinitely and quickly. When Jesus tells Peter that he should forgive seventy times seven, He was actually referring to God's eternal and unending forgiveness. Jesus then gives a picture of compassionate forgiveness. When the master took pity on the servant, he demonstrated a knowledge of empathy, sympathy, and kindness toward his servant. The servant, however, did not immediately learn the lesson of forgiveness that was just given to him. Jesus continues by demonstrating what happens when we do not forgive. When the master learned that the first servant did not extend the same kindness and mercy that he was shown, scripture says that he was handed over to his jailors to be tortured. The final principle demonstrated here is that when we withhold forgiveness, we risk being handed over to our tormentors. Let's be clear, unforgiveness is an open door to the enemy right into our lives. When the enemy comes in, torment follows. The good news is that with repentance, renunciation, healing, and forgiveness, restoration will put us right back on the right path destined by the Lord for our lives. Let's take it one step further. Forgiveness is required for complete physical, mental, and spiritual healing to be received. Look at the end of this book for steps you can take to walk through true biblical forgiveness.

Now that a foundation has been established, let's look at some of the research behind the kingdom principle of forgiveness.

Science says that "when telling of reliving a trauma or wound, your brain is incapable of positive emotion. But our minds can be trained to default to positivity through the practice of forgiveness."[1] Essentially, when we withhold forgiveness and choose to hold a grudge, our minds are designed in such a way that it is impossible to feel positive emotion when describing or remembering the event and moment of the wound or trauma. Think about how your body reacts when reliving a very difficult moment of the past where you were wounded. You might become tense and slightly more frustrated or even angry. Your body might begin to sweat and all you can think about is the hurt and pain. But God made a way through the pain. Emotional, spiritual, and physical healing will begin to occur the moment we choose to release forgiveness.

Forgive and Forget

Have you ever heard the phrase "forgive and forget"? Have you ever said that to yourself? This is possibly one of the most damaging pieces of advice we can tell someone in pain, or even ourselves. Memories are an interesting part of our physical bodies. (We discuss memories in further depth in another chapter.) When trauma or wounding occurs in our lives, the memory is stored in our mind and no amount of attempted forgetting will change that. Try for a moment *not* to think about the last person you spoke to or texted on the phone, and suddenly that will be the thought in the forefront of your mind. You are thinking about a moment in time stored in your memory. Even after forgiveness healing, memories are stored in the mind. But what forgiveness does is remove the pain and trauma of the associated memory. Basically, the memory of the trauma remains, but where pain and hurt used to live, only peace resides now. We forgive and remember peacefully.

God's Way

This book is not glossing over the fact that difficulties do come and go in life. But the good news is that God established principles in forgiveness that bring full restoration. We have a choice where we focus our thoughts and our attention in our daily lives. We can focus on self-hurt and pain, and if we do we open ourselves to more pain and more suffering. But if we choose to broadly distribute forgiveness, we gain clarity and regeneration of our minds, our bodies, and our spirits. Basically, a whole-body healing is received through the exercise of forgiveness.

Biblical principles are amazing; they show us exactly what the command is and what the result will be. For example, Luke 6:38 establishes the principle of giving:

> *Give, and it will be given to you. A good measure, pressed down, shaken together and running over, will be poured into your lap. For with the measure you use, it will be measured to you.*

In other words, "Give [forgiveness], and [forgiveness] will be given to you in abundant measure." Forgiveness healing has the same principles demonstrated in scripture as well.

> *Praise the Lord, my soul; all my inmost being, praise his holy name. Praise the Lord, my soul, and forget not all his benefits—who forgives all your sins and heals all your diseases, who redeems your life from the pit and crowns you with love and compassion, who satisfies your desires with good things so that your youth is renewed like the eagle's (Psalm 103:1-5).*

This is perhaps the best example because it clearly establishes the pattern God uses when we choose to exercise forgiveness. Here we see David praising God and remembering the benefits of God. The principle here is that all healing, redemption, and restoration starts with forgiveness.

The word *benefits* is a great word here. It is the Hebrew word *gmul* (Strong's #H1576), which means "something that aids or promotes well-being." The Bible is saying the benefit of forgiveness is well-being! Here is a breakdown of the principle:

- He forgives first!
- He heals all!
- He redeems you!
- He crowns you with love and compassion!
- He satisfies your desires!
- He renews your youth!

Doesn't it stand to reason that the method that God established should also be used by us? I'm not preaching a formula—as with all things we must partner with the Holy Spirit and allow Him to guide us through all aspects of forgiveness. Principles in scripture are not meant to be formulaic. This is meant to be a spiritual law that, when exercised with the leading of the Holy Spirit, reaps freedom!

In summary, living a forgiveness lifestyle is graduate-level living for believers in Christ. We've learned that forgiveness is a learned practice, made more effective with time and practice. Eventually, walking in forgiveness becomes the norm and the result is a restored life walking in complete healing and freedom.

More Science

We already know that unforgiveness is damaging to our lives. But recent research is showing just how damaging unforgiveness is to our bodies. The following is a simplified breakdown of the research.

To begin, research tells us that unforgiveness leads to elevated stress and causes damage in the following areas:

- Elevated blood pressure
- Elevated heart rate and cortisol levels
- Various mental health problems
- High risk of cardiovascular problems
- Digestive risks
- Immunity risks
- Respiratory problems
- Risk of problems caused to reproductive systems
- Problems in the hippocampus and "other brain structures"[2]
- Arthritis concerns
- Various sleep disorders

Sadly, many people, even those who understand forgiveness, find themselves turning toward and relying on alternate forms of worldly self-therapy in an effort to ease the pain of the past.

> People might try to cope with the disorders, or impending disorders by making lifestyle choices like too much drinking or medication.[3]

These attempts to hide, cover, suppress, and ignore past wounds are at best temporary and at worst causing further damage to our minds and bodies.

Forgiveness Heals

The benefits of forgiveness are becoming widely accepted among the scientific community. Several major university studies have all shown that the practice of forgiveness and even reconciliation has a healing effect on the physical body, emotions, and spirit.

What causes that desire to forgive in even the worst situations? The power of forgiveness to heal cannot be overlooked. The Bible says, "as a man thinks in his heart, so is he" (see Prov. 23:7). If unforgiveness lingers too long, the heart will inevitably grow sick.

Biblically we are commanded to forgive endlessly and refrain from holding on to our bitterness and unforgiveness. What is amazing, though, is how the scientific community actually agrees concerning the benefits of forgiveness therapy. Numerous scientific studies and research have been completed concerning forgiveness benefits to physical health and spiritual health.

Dr. Everett Worthington is Professor Emeritus at Virginia Commonwealth University. He is most regarded for his life work in the area of forgiveness. He is known for developing forgiveness models and has literally written the scientific textbook on forgiveness titled *The Handbook of Forgiveness*. Forgiveness is essential to healing. Dr. Worthington's studies continue to explain the effects of unforgiveness on mental health as well.

Unforgiveness produces rumination (which is unwanted, unregulated, negative emotion-based obsessive thinking). Rumination is related to anger disorders, depression, anxiety, obsessive-compulsive problems, PTSD, and some psychosomatic symptoms. Furthermore, those mental health problems have secondary fallout affecting physical health and relationships.[4]

That all sounds terrible, and complicated, and sadly these are the choices many people are making when they choose not to walk in forgiveness as a lifestyle. Jesus was not instructing the act of forgiveness as an option in Matthew 18:22. Forgiveness is a requirement if we are truly going to live free and effective lives in the kingdom. Moreover, without forgiveness we are walking, talking, hurting, wounded, stress-filled packages of unforgiveness just waiting to either have a blowout or to be truly set free.

I'm not going to pretend that forgiveness is easy, but I am going to tell you it is required for effective, Christ-centered, healthy living. Oh, but good news prevails! Jesus has provided us with the keys to receiving our freedom. Make a choice today to forgive, partner with the Holy Spirit, and allow Him to bring to your mind the events of your life where forgiveness is needed. Then carefully and truly forgive and release each and every hurt, offense, and trauma, allowing your body and mind to heal once and for all.

Recent scientific studies have shown that emotional, mental, and physical healing occur when we operate in a forgiveness lifestyle.

Each scientific study further agrees with biblical principles we discussed earlier. For example, one research study has stated that "beneficial effects of forgiveness [exists] as a psychotherapeutic intervention for many conditions, [such as] PTSD, postabortion grief, and incest."[5] The research continues and delves deeper into the healthy aspects of forgiveness by stating that abnormal brain activations may therefore be amenable to normalization through cognitive intervention, possibly containing a forgiveness component.

That "science" language simply means that the world is now realizing the benefits of forgiveness that the Bible confirmed long ago. That trauma of the past and issues of mental confusion can be fixed by the strategic and intentional use of forgiveness healing.

Mental health is shown to be greatly impacted by forgiveness as shown by recent studies conducted with patients diagnosed with schizophrenia. Patients with this diagnosis have shown an increase in brain activity in certain areas when forgiveness is exercised by the patient. The significance of this study is that schizophrenia patients typically show lower brain activity in these certain areas of the brain when not regularly exercising forgiveness. Essentially this tells us once again just how deep the healing can be when we walk in forgiveness.

Further studies on forgiveness by the Harvard Medical School have concluded that in addition to the positive effects on mental health, forgiveness also heals heart problems; reduces blood pressure; reduces depression, anxiety, and hostility; reduces substance abuse; and promotes higher self-esteem and greater life satisfaction.[6] Conversely, science even shows that suppressed emotions can lead to major health issues in the body including, sadly, an increased mortality rate.[7]

Balance and Approach

It's easy to become fascinated with the research and amazing discoveries and connections to biblical truths. However, we must always operate with balance and with the leading of the Holy Spirit and discernment. Several secular models and methods for forgiveness healing have emerged over the years. While many of them claim great results, there are components that we cannot endorse. One popular method of forgiveness therapy involves deliberately reliving the moment of trauma while exercising empathy for the offender or abuser. The misguided idea here is that if we can understand the moment from the other person's point of view then we are more able to forgive. The error in this is that we should not seek to justify the wrong that was done to a person. The person who wronged you was in the wrong regardless of the intent. Any attempt to justify the abuse or hurt serves to nullify the need for forgiveness by excusing it.

Further models require an "altruistic gift" of forgiveness to be given to the person who wronged you. Again, this is an error. Your forgiveness has nothing to do with the other person, nor is it a gift to that person. The gift of forgiveness is for you. As demonstrated previously, the gift you receive is health, clarity, well-being, and a pain-free past. Furthermore, it is not always possible to reconcile with the person who wronged us. In a perfect world those who caused pain in our lives would admit wrongdoing, change their ways, and seek to reconcile and repair the relationship. However, reconciliation is not always a viable option in circumstances where you have broken away from an unhealthy relationship, or where there was severe or ongoing trauma. Please understand that reconciliation is not required for the principle of forgiveness to be effective in your life. But when reconciliation is possible and does occur, the healing can be powerful, and in some instances more so than forgiveness healing alone.

Who Do We Need to Forgive?

As you read this chapter and learn the immense personal benefit of forgiveness, the Holy Spirit will begin to show you names and faces of people whom you need to forgive. Allow the Holy Spirit to gently bring you to a place where you are ready to forgive and begin the healing process. Who then do we need to forgive? Throughout life we encounter a lot of people. A cursory search of the internet reveals that the average person meets more than 10,000 people in their lifetime and will have interactions with many more. I'm not suggesting that we need to identify every single person throughout your lifetime who wronged you. I am saying that with the partnership of the Holy Spirit, He will bring the impactful moments to your memory so they can be addressed. The people we need to forgive typically fall into the following categories:

- Relationships, parents, family members, relatives, prior or current romantic relationships, children, etc.
- Teachers, professors, instructors

- Friends, acquaintances, social media friends, those who interact with you negatively on social media
- Coworkers, business acquaintances, vendors, customers, bosses
- Traffic offenders, other drivers
- Those who rejected you
- Yourself
- And anyone the Holy Spirit brings to your memory

The causes of a good relationship are abilities to form, maintain, grow, and repair when damaged, a strong emotional bond. Part of the ability to repair damaged emotional bonds includes the ability to forgive.[8]

Forgiveness Is Real

On June 8, 1972, South and North Vietnam were in engaged in intense conflict. The South Vietnamese village of Trảng Bàng was under attack. Fighter pilots were releasing bombs and dropping napalm from aircraft. One South Vietnamese fighter pilot misidentified the citizens in the village below as enemy combatants, and as he flew by he dropped napalm on them as they ran from their homes, from the temple, trying to escape the bombs. Napalm is a sticky and highly flammable material, and it is designed to stick to the body and other objects while intensely burning them.

On that day during this horrible event, a little nine-year-old girl by the name of Phan Thị Kim Phúc was running away with other villagers. You may have heard of her; she is the girl in the famous photo titled "Napalm Girl." She recalls the event with absolute clarity to this day. As she was running away, napalm material was dropped on her. It burned her clothes and her skin. She ran through the street tearing her clothes off yelling "too hot, too hot"[9] because she was covered in so much napalm. Ultimately, 30 percent of her body was burned. The story of her survival is remarkable as she was not expected to live. But God had a plan for redemption. The most impactful story she tells is her journey of forgiveness. As she recounts it today, she recalls:

> The more I prayed for my enemies, the softer my heart became. When I felt real forgiveness, my heart was set free. If I can do it, everyone can do it too.[10]

That part of the story alone is amazing. But allow me to give you little more context. It is important to understand that pilot who dropped the bombs on this village made an error. He was a South Vietnamese pilot bombing what he mistakenly believed was an enemy hideout. Years later, Kim began to discover forgiveness; she began a healing process that involved seeking to find the names of every one of the people who were involved in her terrible experience. Her journey led to intentionally and specifically forgiving the pilot and all the other soldiers involved in the attack. Later, when she was asked how she was able to forgive, she said this:

> "The picture of Jesus Christ when they put Him on the cross and they kill Him, so Jesus say, Father, forgive them, they don't know what they are doing," she replied. "So that picture, that words, Lord, help me to

do the same thing like you did. And I started to pray for my enemies, and the more I prayed for my enemies the softer my heart became."[11]

One day while at a library she discovered and began to read a Bible. She was just trying to make sense of her life. Jesus met her where she was, and through the stories of forgiveness she read in the Bible she saw an opportunity for healing. Also by reading the Bible, she was led to forgiveness and to living a life of renewed purpose and fullness.

Forgiven and Befriended

Chris Carrier was ten years old in 1996 when he was abducted by a stranger and taken into the Everglades. There he was tortured, stabbed multiple times on his body, and stabbed once in his eye. He was burned with cigarettes and finally was shot in the head and left for dead. Miraculously, Chris awoke six days later, walked to the nearest person he could find, and thus survived. Many years later, Chris received notification that his attacker was nearing death and was in the hospital. Many people might not choose to act in the manner Chris did; he visited his attacker in the hospital and began to walk through a personal journey to forgive him for the trauma and wounding he caused. Chris did not wait for his attacker to ask for forgiveness (he never asked). Chris simply understood the principle and chose to forgive and release the man. Chris is alive today, has a family, and is a Christian minister devoted to God.[12]

Just like Kim and Chris and thousands of others with whom we have ministered, you can live a life of healing, purpose, and fullness as well. It begins with the adoption of a lifestyle of forgiveness. Starting now, I encourage you to partner with the Holy Spirit. Allow Him into the hardest places of life. You can trust Him to gently bring complete healing as you walk through your own forgiveness journey. I bless you now, that even as you read this, the Holy Spirit is working on areas in your life that He wants to heal for you. Let Him in and you will never regret it! As you begin this process you might want to refer to the end of this book for a forgiveness healing guide.

NOTES

1. Fred Luskin, *Forgive for Good* (New York, NY: HarperOne, 2002).
2. Everett L. Worthington, Jr., "The Science of Forgiveness," Virginia Commonwealth University Department of Psychology, April 2020, 13, https://www.templeton.org/wp-content/uploads/2020/06/Forgiveness_final.pdf.
3. Ibid.
4. Ibid., 14-15.
5. E.L. Worthington and N.G. Wade, *Handbook of Forgiveness* (Routledge: Taylor & Francis Group, 2020), 264.
6. "The power of forgiveness," Harvard Health Publishing, February 12, 2021, https://www.health.harvard.edu/mind-and-mood/the-power-of-forgiveness.
7. Benjamin P. Chapman, et. al., "Emotion suppression and mortality risk over a 12-year follow-up," *Journal of Psychosomatic Research*, Vol. 75, Issue 4, October 1, 2014, 381–385, https://www.ncbi.nlm.nih.gov/pmc/articles/PMC3939772.
8. Worthington, "The Science of Forgiveness," 13.
9. Nick Ut, "The Terror of War," http://100photos.time.com/photos/nick-ut-terror-war.

10. Reginald Ben-Halliday, "The Story of the Napalm Girl and the Photographer Who Saved Her Life," October 30, 2020, https://historyofyesterday.com/the-story-of-the-napalm-girl-and-the -photographer-who-saved-her-life-5b9f61229d58.

11. Deacon Greg Kandra, "The Powerful Testimony and Conversion of 'The Girl in the Picture,'" Aleteia, April 12, 2016, https://aleteia .org/blogs/aleteia-blog/the-powerful-testimony-and-conversion -of-the-girl-in-the-picture.

12. "Forgiven and Befriended by Victim, Attacker Dies," *New York Times*, October 6, 1996, 34, https://www.nytimes.com/ 1996/10/06/us/forgiven-and-befriended-by-victim-attacker-dies .html.

CHAPTER NINE

INNER HEALING

Is Inner Healing Biblical?

The ministry of inner healing, although somewhat controversial due to the widely varying methods, is easily one of my favorite components of deliverance ministry. We will outline a kingdom-based method in the back of this book. The reason this is one of my favorite processes is because when inner healing is executed properly, the deliverance leader takes an opportunity to step aside and allow Jesus to bring healing and freedom directly to the root. As mature deliverance ministers, we learn the value of quickly getting out of the way and allowing the Holy Spirit to bring freedom. We are there to help the client stay on track, but the healing is done by Jesus.

Put very simply, inner healing is a process of allowing the Holy Spirit to bring up a memory of a time you were wounded. He helps you forgive everyone involved, He helps you identify wrong beliefs you adopted based on what happened in that situation, and He reveals truth so that you can develop new and healthy beliefs.

He ministers directly to you, healing your emotional wounds and removing your pain.

Here is a creative illustration: imagine a bungee cord or rubber band that is connected to the very first trauma or stressful event in your life. This moment might have even occurred within the womb. As you grow older and experience varying stressful or traumatic life events, the cord becomes wrapped around each of those moments throughout life until it is under so much tension that you just can't take it anymore. Finally you realize that deliverance ministry and inner healing have become a necessity. The enemy greatly enjoys playing with your vulnerabilities and he loves tugging on that already high-tension cord in your life. Ultimately, when a person receives the ministry of inner healing, we watch as the Holy Spirit comes right in and unhooks the cord from just the right root or trauma in their life, releasing the tension and setting them free in an instant!

We have a double victory when this happens. First, Jesus removes the tension that bound the person and held them captive in slavery. And second, their life is restored. Once all pain associated with trauma and mistakes of the past has been removed, the individual will have the capacity and freedom to get traction in life, to walk in purpose and destiny as a victorious son or daughter of God.

In today's culture and ministry environment it is increasingly important that we back up our ministry techniques with biblical foundations. I believe Jesus is and always will be the foundation (see 1 Cor. 3:11 AMP). I also believe we build on that foundation as we remain in relationship with Jesus, and He continues the process of bringing revelation and fresh ideas. Inner healing is one area where the Lord has continually given us more revelation, and we have gradually updated our methods accordingly. When we partner with the Holy Spirit in inner healing, captives are set free. The freedom received frequently occurs in both the past and present time. God is outside the limits of space and time, and therefore He is able to heal a wound in the very moment it was sustained.

Healing Deep Wounds

He heals the brokenhearted and binds up their wounds [curing their pains and their sorrows] (Psalm 147:3 AMPC).

This verse demonstrates that Jesus heals the brokenhearted and binds wounds. We're not just talking about present concerns. Issues of a broken heart occur over time and can involve multiple traumas causing deep spiritual, physical, and mental wounds that require Jesus' personal touch. The word *brokenhearted* in this verse is the Hebrew word *shabar,* which means "to be torn into pieces and crushed" (Strong's #H7665). Inner healing, when done properly, is a solemn and intimate time with the Lord inviting Him to bring the shattered pieces back together and removing all the associated pain. He does not just heal the broken pieces; this verse clearly says that He also binds up the wounds. The word *bind* comes from the word *chabash,* which means "to gird up and to heal" (Strong's #H2280). This is where things become interesting. The word *gird* means "to be surrounded and enclosed." This word also means "to be prepared for battle." This verse is essentially guiding us through the inner healing process in a very basic way.

Discover the Lie and Replace with Truth

And you will know the Truth, and the Truth will set you free (John 8:32 AMPC).

Discovering and understanding the demonic lies in our lives and coming into agreement with God's perfect truth is probably the most important component when it comes to ministering and receiving inner healing. We already know that satan is the father of lies. So it would stand to reason that his demon minions strive to emulate his example. They are professional liars and thieves. Their purpose is to steal, kill, and destroy your life, and one of their favorite methods is by way of your beliefs.

The thief comes only to steal and kill and destroy; I have come that they may have life, and have it to the full (John 10:10).

If a tormenting demonic spirit can coerce you to come into agreement with a lie concerning your purpose and identity, it wins. But through partnership with the Holy Spirit and your God-given gift of discernment you can identify the lie. And once the lie is revealed it only takes an instant to become awakened to the manifest truth that will reveal the hope and future God desires for you. Then, once you identify and accept the truth, the lie dissolves and you become free and unbound as the enemy's grasp over you dissolves in a moment. This principle of seeking truth, wisdom, and understanding is first established in Proverbs 23:23. The lies of the enemy cannot stand against truth. When Jesus was tormented in the desert, the only weapon He needed was to speak truth. Every time He said the words, "It is written," He was speaking truth that satan was unable to overcome even with his greatest lies and temptations.

> *Buy the truth and do not sell it—wisdom, instruction and insight as well* (Proverbs 23:23).

Forgiveness Is Required

> *Then Peter came to Him and said, "Lord, how often shall my brother sin against me, and I forgive him? Up to seven times?" Jesus said to him, "I do not say to you, up to seven times, but up to seventy times seven"* (Matthew 18:21–22 NKJV).

Deliverance begins with forgiveness; Jesus is making it clear that we are to infinitely forgive. In this verse Jesus is providing a depth of teaching that it takes heavenly wisdom to fully grasp. Simply put, Jesus was making it clear to Peter that we are not to place limits on forgiveness. For the sake of our own lives, our health, and that of our generational lineage, our deliverance must always begin with forgiveness. Forgiveness was addressed in-depth in the preceding chapter. Look toward the end of the book for our biblically based model for forgiveness healing.

Matthew 18:21–35 then becomes our framework for forgiveness ministry. Jesus' command to us is to continuously and mercifully forgive just as the master forgave his attendant of his debt and spared his family. Jesus uses the equation of seventy times seven concerning how many times we should forgive someone. The number 490 in Hebrew is the alphanumeric word *tamim*, which means "blameless, complete, and full of integrity."

Essentially, Jesus is telling us that in the act of forgiveness we become blameless, complete, and ones with integrity. Jesus is not presenting a "nice to know" message of forgiveness here. He is not just talking about the guy in the green Corvette who cut you off on the highway this morning or the person at the office who drank the last of the coffee. Jesus is speaking to every moment of offense, wounding, hurt, and trauma that, if left undealt with, opens the door to the enemy to steal your healing.

There is more at stake here than taking the high road and being obedient. In verses 32–34 the master catches his servant acting in merciless unforgiveness by refusing to extend forgiveness to his own peer servant who owed him money. The servant is literally turned over to his tormentors to have their way with him. If we allow ourselves to hold unforgiveness in our hearts, we are burying any opportunity for healing both at the spiritual and physical levels. Further, we are allowing our tormentors (demonic assignments) to come right into our lives and minds to take up residence.

If inner healing is going to work, it requires forgiveness of those who have wounded us. Additionally, Mark 11:25 (AMP) makes it clear that every time we pray, we are to forgive and let it go. I have learned by way of experience and a little science that physical and spiritual healing cannot manifest fully if unforgiveness exists.

So based on these scriptures, we minister inner healing. First the presence and glory of the Holy Spirit is welcome and fills the room even at the moment of wounding and trauma. Forgiveness follows with sincerely releasing the abusers (and sometimes forgiving and releasing yourself) to the Lord. The next thing is partnering with the Holy Spirit, asking Him to identify the lies you began to believe due to the hurt you sustained in that situation, and then reveal the truth that will replace those lies. Jesus then begins to restore the broken pieces of your heart and gird you, hold you, surround you, and envelop you with the truth of your identity as a son or daughter of the King. From there the healing washes over your body and all pain from the moment of original wounding is released and you are free! This process is not spooky spiritual; it is biblical. It is supernatural and it is a real demonstration of the power of God that cannot be denied. The final chapter of this book will cover in detail the method we use to minister inner healing, so you can use it for yourself.

One note of caution: while you can safely take yourself through inner healing, only someone who has been properly trained should attempt to take another person through inner healing. There is great potential for damage to your clients if you attempt to administer this method without proper knowledge. This is because it is easy for a third party to interfere while attempting to assist, and the power of suggestion introduced by the minister can skew the client's memories and their healing experience. However, individuals are welcome to use the methods in this book for their own personal needs as often as they meet with the Lord.

Distorted Memories?

There is a growing population of lay counselors and licensed clinical therapists who believe that memory recollection is irreparably flawed. The belief is that each time a memory is recalled it is altered and becomes far too distorted to be of any reliable use. As stated by Dr. Philip Gold, "Human memory is inherently faulty.

At best, memories are selective: totally true but not the total truth. They also change over time."[1]

These memories are known as pseudo memories that over time become a partially or greatly incorrect memory. In the last decade of deliverance ministry, I have seen numerous occasions where "new" memories suddenly surface causing the client to seek deliverance and healing. As a minister this is a delicate issue; we are not licensed therapists and as such must only address the potential demonic stronghold and inner healing as we are guided by the Holy Spirit. In other situations, we encounter people who have seen other ministries or even other therapists who have used the power of suggestion to infer the possibility of prior abuse or trauma. Such action on the part of anyone in ministry or professional therapy is abhorrent. When people come for ministry, they are trusting in our ability to use discretion, discernment, prophetic insight, and the leading of the Holy Spirit to guide everything we say and do. Where a licensed therapist is concerned, they are trusted to have professional judgment not to lead or use the power of suggestion with a vulnerable client.

I have personally mistered to individuals fitting both of these categories. It is fairly common for female clients to describe a sudden dream or memory of someone close, perhaps a father, molesting her at a very young age. In every instance, we acknowledge the sadness of the memory without validating it at this stage. Likewise, I have ministered to women who come to me stating that they were told by their therapist or other minister that they "may" have been sexually molested as a child. And since the time they were told these things, memories began appearing confirming the suggestions. I am not stating emphatically that all sudden memories are false or incorrect. What I am stating is that with all new memory recollection we must be discerning and proceed with great caution so as not to damage our clients further. If I validate a memory and decide of my own volition to take the client into inner healing for that trauma, I am solidifying that memory and essentially agreeing that it is reality. The result is a person who came into my office with a potential recollection and left with validation of an event that may have never happened. Or it may have happened, but perhaps the memory is not completely accurate. Remember, memories become distorted and altered over time. It is for this reason that we only address inner healing as guided by the Holy Spirit and only when the memory is brought to mind by Him.

Mistakes Made When Working with Memories

A woman walked into our office to receive deliverance prayer. We sat down and before I could open the session, the woman began to explain to the team that she had just recently had vague dreams suggesting inappropriate touching by a family member when she was a baby. In that moment I was faced with a "go" or "no-go" decision. If I chose to administer inner healing by asking her to go into that memory, I would essentially be saying that I agreed the dream was based on a real memory. That is a dangerous path as we have no way of validating a person's memories, much less their dreams. I am not suggesting that her dream had no truth; I am, however, stating that we must discern with complete accuracy what the *Lord* wants to do next. I chose to acknowledge the woman's memory but stopped short of validating it.

Allow me to elaborate a bit concerning the improper ways inner healing is sometimes administered.

As ministers we often meet with people like the one mentioned above. They may tell us stories they remember from their childhood. They may elaborate on how their father was verbally abusive or their mother was distant and a grandfather or uncle was always there for them when they needed them. As the individual recounts their story, they suddenly begin to feel like something might not have been right concerning relationships with their grandfather or the uncle. In this hypothetical scenario the minister might lean into this train of thinking and suggest that some form of inappropriate relationship may have taken place. At that moment, the minister has planted the seed of an idea by making a leading suggestion to the individual based on conjecture rather than facts. This person may walk out of the ministry session more damaged than when she entered. Even if healing prayer was performed, the memory was validated rather than allowing the Holy Spirit to guide the person to the actual memory that needed healing and restoration.

I am not suggesting that memories should be ignored or pushed to the side. On the contrary, we must allow the Holy Spirit to be the guide and *only* the memories He brings to mind are the ones we are to submit to Him for healing. We can trust that the Holy Spirit will be faithful to bring up the exact thing that needs to be dealt with, and He will never push a person to deal with something for which they are not ready. If you are confused about the method of inner healing I am describing, not to worry—you will find our methods in the final chapter of this book.

Inner Healing Done Correctly

I once prayed alongside a well-known deliverance minister as we ministered inner healing to an individual who we will call Suzie (we will not use her real name for privacy purposes). In this session, as usual, we asked the Holy Spirit to bring to Suzie's mind a memory that He would like to heal. Almost immediately Suzie began to recall with vivid clarity a scene that could have only occurred several hundred years prior. Suzie described the event from the perspective of a little child who was frightened and watching a terrible scene break out on a ship at sea, involving several grown men engaged in a violent sword fight. That would have been a frightening scene for a child who was likely watching a traumatic event impacting someone very close. As the memory played out in great detail, we began to wonder if this was an actual event or a false recollection, because it had obviously not occurred in her own life. But as Suzie continued, it became clear that this event was strangely close to home and was impacting her in such an emotional way that we could not deny that God was revealing to her a generational trauma that needed healing at the DNA level. Additionally, we had confidence the memory was indeed true because we had specifically invited the Holy Spirit to bring a memory to Suzie's recollection. The healing that transpired as we followed and watched the Holy Spirit minister to Suzie was miraculous, live-giving, and restorative.

This story illustrates the need for mature inner healing ministers who can discern the Holy Spirit from a distorted or even false memory.

Responsibly led inner healing ministry will not engage a sudden recollection of a dream or a word given by a less experienced prophet or seer. The problem with a sudden recollection is that there are too many variables that could influence a memory. We've already discussed the power of suggestion and influence we have over people's memory. Additionally, during inner healing, the session is covered by the blood of Jesus and we forbid any voice other than the voice of the Lord to influence memory recollection. Inner healing will always prepare a special time with the Lord, allowing Him to heal what is needed. I have learned through years of experience that sudden or suggested memories are almost never brought to mind when we allow Jesus to run the session. This is important because we are not ignoring the sudden memory, we are simply turning the session over to the Holy Spirit and if He wants to work on that memory, He does. Nearly every time, the memory the client thought needed healing when they came to us was not truly the root Jesus wanted to heal.

Can We Identify Distorted Memories?

In a perfect world we would be able to identify distortions in memory. However, we don't possess the capability to easily discern true memory events from distortions.

Memory distortion and flawed recollection is known as memory confabulation. *Confabulation* is defined in *Webster's Dictionary* as filling in gaps in memory by fabrication. As a minister of inner healing and deliverance, the best way to prevent memory confabulation during ministry is to plead the blood of Jesus and forbid the enemy from interfering. Then permit the Holy Spirit free rein to influence true memory recollection. When properly done, inner healing is an incredible mechanism where Jesus sets the captives free in an instant. All it takes is for us as ministers to step aside and let the Lord have His way.

Rewire, but Never Change the Memory

Now that we are familiar with memory distortions and confabulation as it relates to memory recollection, let's discuss rewiring the memory. This is perhaps the wrong word for what is actually happening. In truth, memories are not altered in any way. What occurred in the past is locked in history and can never be changed. Some improper inner healing practices have involved altering or erasing the memory during the healing session. For example, we should never ask the individual to move to a different area in their memory or specifically ask Jesus to walk into the place where the event occurred during the recollection. Any attempt to change the memory in any way is incorrect and manipulative of the vulnerable client. Consider the potential damage this can cause a person who is reliving a trauma of the past, seeking healing when we invite Jesus into the room. I have heard clients who have experienced this type of inner healing say, "If Jesus is able to visit me during this trauma, why did He not save me back when it actually happened? He could have saved me and instead stood by."

Instead, rewiring of the memory refers to the moment when God reveals the lie that was born out of the trauma, replaces it with truth, and removes the pain associated with the memory. Welcoming the presence of the Holy Spirit into the ministry room to bring peace, truth, and comfort is appropriate and important to the healing process.

Note: while much of this section deals with ministers working with clients for their inner healing needs, the process of inner healing is something we all can do safely on our own as we meditate with the Lord regularly. Bring your traumas to the Lord and allow Him to uncover the lie, reveal the truth, and remove the pain. This practice can be performed alone between just you and Jesus.

Memory Storage and Recollection

We just learned how memories can become distorted and inaccurate over time. Let's look deeper at this phenomenon as we attempt to understand the complexity of inner healing.

Let's start by explaining briefly how our memories work. Essentially memories are part of our physical human comprehension. The memory process is designed to provide us with recall of prior events and as a method with which to weigh our current environment. Research shows that there are three main ways to characterize how memory works. First, the memory encoding process; next, the storage process; followed by the retrieval process.

The encoding process is how we take information into our minds for storage. We encode memories through our senses. How something looks, feels, sounds, etc. is processed and stored. But "the form in which this information is stored may differ from its original encoded form." This is one reason false memory fragments occur requiring the Holy Spirit to guide us through the healing process. Addressing the false or fragments of memory can cause unintended damage during the healing process, potentially even stalling the healing. The storage process determines how the memory is cataloged and stored. Memories will either find a home in long-term storage or short-term storage. All memories are first stored in short-term memory, only moving it to long-term storage if the memory has an associated word, phrase, video, picture, event, etc. This encoding process is called semantic encoding. Finally, the retrieval process of memory refers to the recall process of stored memories. Memory "retrieval is subject to error, because it can reflect a reconstruction of memory. The reconstruction becomes necessary when stored information is lost over time due to decayed retention."[2]

You might think that memories are stored neatly on a shelf or a filing cabinet in our mind waiting to be remembered at a later time. In fact, it's much more complicated than that. Memories are stored in the mind in different places of the cortex depending on the stress of the trauma and emotion associated with it. To further complicate things, memory recollection can be broken causing partial or complete forgetfulness of a memory.[3] For example, the amygdala is responsible for storing the emotional aspects of the memory, then, in partnership with the hypothalamus, communication is sent to the endocrine system to distribute hormones that lead to elevated stress and feelings of discomfort. This is why the retelling or reliving of a trauma memory often triggers physical reactions, heart rate increase, sweating, etc. The other portions of the memory are tucked away in the hippocampus for long-term storage. This is where things get interesting. High-stress memories stored in the hippocampus are potentially subject to a previously introduced phenomenon called confabulation. According to neuroscientist Dr. Dalla Barba, "Confabulation is a kind of memory distortion, that, at a general level, can be defined as the production of statements or actions that are unintentionally incongruous to the subject's history, background, present and future situation."[4] Essentially, memories stored in high-trauma situations are at risk of distortion and misrepresentation at the point of memory recollection. The hippocampus will add and interpret data from previous and current life experience when recalling a memory.

Again, it is for this reason that inner healing should never be performed outside of the secured covering of the Holy Spirit guiding the recollection with accuracy.

Our Vision Is Fallible

I am spending a lot of time addressing memory storage and recollection in this book for a reason. If we have a somewhat thorough understanding of how memories operate, we are better able to approach inner healing, both as a client and as a minister.

"If I can see it, I can believe it." Have you ever said that? Have you ever relied on your vision as the source of all truth? Have you ever maintained a memory of a place or an event from childhood only to discover in pictures that things were not the way you recalled? Often, we discover evidence that makes it apparent our recollection was not entirely accurate.

It might turn out the people involved were different than who we thought, objects might not be the same size as we remember, or other aspects we thought we remembered quite vividly might be wrong. For example, I recently had a desire to look up the childhood home in which I spent many of my elementary school years growing up. This memory is several decades old. I remembered a moderately sized home with a big deck on the front. I remembered there being a large tree in front of the home with a wraparound driveway. I remembered the inside had three average-sized bedrooms—two bedrooms on the main level and one very large attic bedroom—plus a kitchen and dining room combo and a moderate living room. I also remembered a large laundry room that also served as a mudroom at the back door. I remembered a big backyard with a very mature oak tree in the middle of the yard. Strangely, I still remember the street address with perfect clarity. I began searching for this address in Google maps. The address I recalled was correct. But as I began to observe the street view photos, I was shocked to discover several things that don't exactly reconcile with my memory. First, the house is much smaller than I remember. There is a small tree in the backyard, probably an elm tree. And the backyard was much smaller and differently shaped than I remember. There was no wraparound driveway, nor was there any room for one.

While I had strong emotions about what I thought was a vivid memory of my childhood house, reality was vastly different. Dr. Steven Novella of the Yale School of Medicine says this, "The brain is our universal tool and greatest strength. Most people believe that our intelligence is our greatest advantage over all the other creatures on this planet. However, the brain is also strangely deceptive and is the root of many of our flaws and weaknesses." He continues to state the following concerning our vision: "You cannot trust anything you think you see or perceive. There are simply too many flaws in the ways our brain constructs these perceptions."[5]

You Cannot Trust Your Eyes

One of the strangest phenomena concerning human sight is that our eyes are designed with a visual impairment that science may view as a flaw. Or is it? Human eyes have what is called a natural scotoma, a blind spot in both eyes where we are completely incapable of sight. This phenomenon occurs as a result of where the optic nerve exits the retina. There are no photoreceptors to transmit light from this area. You could draw the conclusion that we are partially blind in both eyes. In fact, our blind spot is unusually large when compared to our entire field of vision. That's remarkable! Think about this for a moment.

> *Therefore we are always confident and know that as long as we are at home in the body we are away from the Lord. For we live by faith, not by sight* (2 Corinthians 5:6-7).

We live by faith and not by sight. Why then, you might ask, do I have no problem seeing? And why do I not notice that large of a gap in my vision? Truthfully, the answer is entirely the result of the creativity of our God. He knit us together in the secret place; He created a mind so well built that it literally fills in the empty spot with data obtained from surrounding images. Here is the implication: every memory stored in your mind has a blind spot where no data was recorded. As our mind retells the story of a memory, it is doing it without the benefit of current, accurate data to fill in the spot. The potential is a partially distorted memory. I hope you can see why inner healing is so important but also requires so much care of the person to allow the Holy Spirit to heal memories that we cannot begin to understand with complete accuracy.

God Is Everywhere: Omnipresent Healing at the Point of Injury and at the Present

Praise the Lord, my soul; all my inmost being, praise his holy name. Praise the Lord, my soul, and forget not all his benefits—who forgives all your sins and heals all your diseases (Psalm 103:1–3).

God exists out of time and space. He literally inhabits eternity, as beautifully written in Isaiah 57:15. God's presence is always present and among us. Imagine for a moment what life would be like even for a small period of time that God's presence was not here. Horror? Terror? Hopelessness? Let's not explore that further, shall we? The point is that God inhabits eternity. Don't take my word for it; let's look at the following scriptures that illustrate God's ever presence.

> *Have I not commanded you? Be strong and courageous. Do not be afraid; do not be discouraged, for the Lord your God will be with you wherever you go* (Joshua 1:9).
>
> *Be strong and courageous. Do not be afraid or terrified because of them, for the Lord your God goes with you; he will never leave you nor forsake you* (Deuteronomy 31:6).
>
> *The Lord your God is with you, the Mighty Warrior who saves. He will take great delight in you; in his love he will no longer rebuke you, but will rejoice over you with singing* (Zephaniah 3:17).
>
> *Therefore go and make disciples of all nations, baptizing them in the name of the Father and of the Son and of the*

Holy Spirit, and teaching them to obey everything I have commanded you. And surely I am with you always, to the very end of the age (Matthew 28:19–20).

Why then do we hear the church pray for the presence of the Lord? Perhaps because we desire a greater, more tangible manifestation? I acknowledge that "Jesus bumps" are nice, and that is certainly one manifestation. But it starts by acknowledging that God's presence is already here and welcoming Him to come and partner more deeply with the healing that is taking place in the moment. Jesus desires to heal broken places in our lives. When we acknowledge His presence during inner healing, we also invite Him to go deep into the trauma of the memory to remove all pain and wounding associated with the trauma. Jesus is able to remove all pain associated because He inhabits all eternity. Your memory is part of His eternity. When we invite Him to heal a wound, we also ask God to speak truth and peace in the precious and sacred healing moment. This moment is the same moment where miracles happen. When Jesus speaks truth and peace, both truth and peace become the reality, and the pain of the trauma is erased in a moment.

As a reminder, inner healing will never change or alter a memory in any way. Doing so is dangerous and has the potential to cause more damage. But when inner healing is led by the Holy Spirit and discernment, the result is a life lived in freedom, peace, and renewed identity.

Notes

1. Philip Gold, "False memory syndrome," (Salem Press Encyclopedia, 2020), https://search.ebscohost.com/login.aspx?direct=true&AuthType=shib&db=ers&AN=87322551&site=eds-live&custid=uphoenix.

2. Derek Bok Center, "How Memory Works," Harvard University, accessed July 2, 2021, https://bokcenter.harvard.edu/how-memory-works.

3. Greg Miller, "How Are Memories Stored and Retrieved?" *Science*, Vol. 309, Issue 5731, July 1, 2005, 92, https://pubmed.ncbi.nlm.nih.gov/15994538.

4. Gianfranco Dalla Barba and Valentina La Corte, A "neurophenomenological model for the role of the hippocampus in temporal consciousness. Evidence from confabulation," *Frontiers in Behavioral Neuroscience*, Vol. 9, Issue 218, August 26, 2015, https://www.ncbi.nlm.nih.gov/pmc/articles/PMC4549641.

5. Steven Novella, *Your Deceptive Mind: A Scientific Guide to Critical Thinking Skills* (Teaching Company, 2012).

CHAPTER TEN

HOW TO RECEIVE AND MINISTER FREEDOM

We have inundated you with information thus far to give you an understanding of how physical, mental, and spiritual health are all intertwined. The question now becomes, what can you do with that information?

While there are healthcare experts and mental health professionals to utilize as needed, how do you address the spiritual side of this equation? That is where this chapter comes in. We will help you put to use what you have read here with simple tools that are both systematic *and* Holy-Spirit led.

A couple of key notes: when we pray out loud, we release God's power into the earth and into our own bodies. He designed it to work that way when He gave mankind dominion over the earth. Therefore, when we pray in the ministry of deliverance, we are primarily making decrees (as opposed to asking Jesus to do something). We can do this because we decree in accordance with the written word of God in the Bible, in agreement with His stated desires. We do not need to beg Him to set us free, because He has already stated, *"It is for freedom that Christ has set us free"* (Gal. 5:1

NIV). We do not need to beg for forgiveness because, *"If we confess our sins, he is faithful and just and will forgive us our sins and purify us from all unrighteousness"* (1 John 1:9). We must simply repent (turn away from it and go the other direction) and then accept the forgiveness He has already offered. The asking part comes in asking the Holy Spirit for wisdom, strategy, revelation, and inviting God to do whatever He wants in and through us. When we cast out a demon, we are not asking God to remove it but speaking directly to the evil spirit and telling it to leave in the name and authority of Jesus. We can ask God to send angelic help to enforce the commands we are speaking out to the demon.

As far as the "order of operations," so to speak, for these tools, we recommend the following. Go through:

- (If needed) Tool 1.1: Prayer of Salvation
- (If needed) Tool 1.2: Prayer to Be Filled with the Holy Spirit
- Tool 2.1: Prayer Inviting God's Deliverance Power
- Tool 8.1: Forgiveness Healing Method

After this, go back to Tool 3.1 and work through the remaining tools sequentially.

As you go through the various steps, you may find that painful memories surface. When this happens, use Tool 9.1: Inner Healing Method. You can return to inner healing as many times as you need to. You may also think of additional people you need to forgive, and you should return to Tool 8.1: Forgiveness Healing Method as many times as needed. Because people will continue to wound us from time to time, inner healing and forgiveness are things you will need to return to over the rest of your life.

INTRODUCTION

Tool 1.1: Prayer of Salvation

While we would like to assume that every person reading this book has accepted Jesus as their Savior, we know that may not be the case. Nothing you have read here will bring true and lasting freedom without that foundation, because all freedom comes through Jesus and the work He did on the cross!

To clarify:

- Baptism is not salvation
- Christening is not salvation
- Baby dedication is not salvation
- Growing up in church is not salvation
- Being raised in a Christian home or culture is not salvation
- Believing there is a God and trying to be a moral person is not salvation

So then, what *is* salvation? The Bible says, *"If you declare with your mouth, 'Jesus is Lord,' and believe in your heart that God raised him from the dead, you will be saved"* (Rom. 10:9).

Instructions for Individuals

If you have never done so before, then pray the following prayer out loud. Mean it with your heart, and know that God awaits you with open arms!

Instructions for Ministers

More than once we have been ministering to a person and found they never accepted Jesus as their Savior. We have had to stop in the middle of the ministry session and lead them through a prayer of salvation. This is something to be watchful of. It is best to ask the client at the outset about their conversion experience, about how their life changed afterward, and how they spend time with the Lord in daily life. When someone says, "My parents told me I asked Jesus into my heart when I was two years old, but I don't remember it," or "I don't know, I guess I've always gone to church," or "I was baptized into the church as an infant," those types of statements are clues that the person may need to be led to the Lord before you proceed with further ministry.

Prayer of Salvation

> *Father God, I acknowledge that I am a sinner and that my sin has separated me from You. I love You, and I confess that You are the one true God. I believe You sent Your Son Jesus to die on the cross to pay the penalty for my sins. I believe Jesus rose from the dead on the third day, conquering sin and death, and making a way for*

me to be reunited with You! Jesus, I acknowledge You as Lord, and I ask You to be in charge of my life. I commit to following Your ways. I want to be Your son/daughter, to be Your servant, and to be Your friend. Holy Spirit, come and inhabit me now. Thank You for cleansing me, adopting me, and making me a new creation!

Tool 1.2: Prayer to Be Filled with the Holy Spirit

Once again, this is basic but too important to work based on the assumption that everyone "already knows." When you become saved, the Holy Spirit inhabits you. But there is also a pouring out of His power that we refer to as being "filled with the Holy Spirit," and some may also call it being "baptized in the Holy Spirit." This is a separate event, and while it does not affect salvation, it absolutely affects your ability to relate to God, to feel His presence, receive His love, and to function in the calling He has placed on your life. It is necessary even to correctly interpret and apply scripture, as the Bible says the Holy Spirit is our teacher.

Many people relate being filled with the Holy Spirit to speaking in tongues. We do believe the personal prayer language iteration of speaking in tongues is immediately available when you become filled with the Holy Spirit. We also believe this is only *one* of the manifestations of the Holy Spirit, and certainly not the only one! All of the spiritual gifts listed in the Bible are manifestations of His infilling. If you speak in tongues right away, that is wonderful! If that comes a bit later, do not be worried; it will come in God's timing. The evidence you should look for immediately is to see an increase of the power and anointing in your life, your ability to serve others through various spiritual gifts, and your ability to hear God's voice.

The only thing you need to do in order to be filled with the Holy Spirit is to ask!

Instructions for Individuals

If you have never done so, pray the following prayer out loud. Mean it with your heart and be in expectation that the Holy Spirit is eager to fill you to overflowing!

Instructions for Ministers

It is best to ask clients early on about whether they have been filled with the Holy Spirit, and what evidence they have seen of this in their lives. If they have not had this experience, ask if they are willing to pray this prayer now. This will greatly increase their spiritual discernment and their openness to receive from God, which makes it much easier for them to receive freedom during the ministry time. You may want to help them initiate their prayer language, but that is not the main goal and don't get hung up on it. People sometimes freeze up if they feel pressured. Follow the Holy Spirit's leading!

Prayer to Be Filled with the Holy Spirit

Holy Spirit, just like You did for the disciples in Acts chapter 2, I invite You to come and fill me with Your presence and Your power! I welcome You. I receive everything You have for me! Fill me so that I can be an instrument of Yours, overflowing with Your love and Your power. I invite You to give me a prayer language of tongues, and

I invite You to give me every spiritual gift that You want to flow from me. Thank You! Amen!

TOOLS FROM CHAPTER 2

PHYSICAL FREEDOM THROUGH SPIRITUAL DELIVERANCE

Tool 2.1: Prayer Inviting God's Deliverance Power

And I will do whatever you ask in my name, so that the Father may be glorified in the Son. You may ask me for anything in my name, and I will do it (John 14:13-14).

The point of becoming free is not merely so that we can feel better (although we do). It is so that we can walk with God unhindered, receive from Him freely, serve Him effectively, minister to others, and so that His name will be glorified through all of this!

Every person wanting to be delivered should begin by asking the Lord to do so.

Before you utilize any of the other tools in this book, pray the prayer below out loud. You can personalize it as much as you want. Pray it from your heart.

Prayer

*Father God, I come into agreement with Your desire for
me to be free. Jesus, I acknowledge You as my Savior and
Lord. I accept Your forgiveness for every sin of mine. I
choose to turn away from every sin; teach me to walk in
righteousness! I choose to forgive myself just as Christ
has forgiven me. I forgive all who sinned against me
in any way. Lord, I invite You to cleanse me, align my
thoughts with Yours, heal my emotions and physical
body, and remove anything from me that is a hindrance
in my relationship with You. I trust You, Holy Spirit,
and give You full permission to do whatever You want to
do, however You want to do it. Thank You for Your love
and for rescuing me from every evil attack! I now cancel
every assignment of the enemy against me and command every evil spirit to leave me now and go directly
to a dry and arid place, never to return! In the mighty
name of Jesus, amen!*

EPIGENETICS, DNA, AND DEMONS

I n this segment we equip you to break off the curses and demonic attachments that have impacted your DNA due to direct or inherited sin or trauma.

Read the following prayer out loud, with authority and from your heart.

Tool 3.1: DNA Healing and Reset Prayer

I thank You, Lord, that I am fearfully and wonderfully made. I acknowledge and declare what Your word says: that I am created in Your likeness, that I am created to be perfect, that You called me to represent Your kingdom on earth.

I acknowledge actions and choices have opened doors and invited the enemy into our family lineage. In the name of Jesus, I renounce all familiar, generational spirits that have been assigned to my lineage, and every way they have manifested in my life or my family line. I repent of all involvement with every evil spirit and command them to leave me now!

I repent for all ungodly actions that I have participated in that caused trauma to another person, as a result contributing to my own bloodline DNA corruption.

I repent for all ungodly actions that I have participated in that caused trauma in my own body, thereby marking my own gene code with the trauma.

I forgive myself for all ungodly actions that have created trauma in both myself and others, leaving marks on their genetic code and mine.

I forgive all others who have harmed me and who have changed my genetic code as a result of the trauma and stress I endured or inherited.

I repent for saying and believing that I am the result of my ancestral genes and as such am a flawed person by design.

I repent for coming into agreement with genetic infirmity and I choose to accept the truth that I am created in the image of God as it is written in Genesis 1:27.

I renounce all curses, oaths, and false prophecies that are attached to my family bloodline.

I renounce all oaths taken by me or anyone throughout my entire family lineage.

I renounce the lie that I am the result of my inherited genes. I now declare that my genes and my DNA do not *define me. I declare that I am perfectly and wonderfully made according to Psalm 139:14.*

I renounce all infirmities inherited through my bloodline.

I renounce the argument of nature versus nurture. I am not a statistic and my body and mind will not be held captive in earthly bondages. I declare I am more than what science says I am.

I declare that I no longer choose to conform to the patterns of this world, and therefore I reject all attempts of the enemy to alter or change my DNA for ungodly purposes.

I break all attachments that my ancestors or I invited into my blood, my DNA, and my genes as a result of ungodly sexual involvements.

I break all trauma brought on my genetic code as a result of any sexual molestation or rape.

I break all changes to my DNA as a result of my willing participation in ungodly sexual practices, including sex before marriage, adultery, pornography (both as a viewer and a participant), homosexuality, bestiality, BDSM, or sex with incubus and succubus or any other demon spirit.

I now command all epigenetic marks on my DNA that attached themselves during traumatic experiences that occurred everywhere in my family lineage to the tenth generation to immediately be removed and to leave my body now!

I command my DNA to immediately forget all epigenetic marks brought on through trauma and ungodly involvements and to immediately reset—to begin perfectly replicating once again according to how my body was intended by God according to Psalm 139:14–16.

I now command my genes to switch off the results from all inherited trauma brought on me as a result of generational curses and familial spirits attached to my lineage.

I command each of the 92 telomeres in each of the 30 trillion DNA chromosomes in my body to be lengthened and strengthened right now in the name of Jesus.

I command all memories contained within my hippocampus and my amygdala to become whole and to represent each event with complete accuracy. Lord, I ask You to cleanse my mind of all false memories and all false fragments of my memory leaving only the truth of each event intact.

God, it is written that when we ask You for healing, we will receive! Therefore, I now ask You, Lord, for a complete and thorough reset of my entire genetic code returning me to the perfection You intended at creation. And now, Lord, I declare Proverbs 17:22 over myself, "A cheerful heart is good medicine." I choose to have a spirit of joy that brings healing to my body.

Thank You, Lord, for my complete healing!

THE SCIENCE OF FEAR

Overcoming the Spirit of Fear

In Chapter Four we addressed the science behind the spirit of fear. What follows is a guide as you walk through your own personal freedom from the spirit of fear. Never again allow the demonic stronghold of fear manipulate, debilitate, or suppress your life. The power to overcome fear begins with a personal relationship with Jesus Himself, because Jesus is perfect love, and perfect love casts out all fear. Begin your freedom journey using the process outlined below as a place to begin.

How to Overcome Fear and Anxiety and Walk in Peace

The steps outlined below are not intended to be linear in practice. Instead, as you spend time developing your relationship with Jesus, He will guide you appropriately. There is nothing wrong with a linear approach; just don't make it the rule.

Submit to Effective Deliverance Ministry

We encourage you to find a biblically sound deliverance ministry to help you take authority over fears and demonic attachments in your life.

Participate in Regular Social Community with People Who Support You

Hebrews 10:24–25 provides guidance concerning our participation with other believers. Some of you may want to think outside of the box and seek God concerning what your "community" looks like. We have typically understood this scripture to be referring to a local church. It can be a church certainly! But it can also be any group of believers who carry the love and passion of Jesus. Many of these groups are called apostolic centers, or micro churches, or even home churches. God is changing the construct of the traditional church and is breaking down old mindsets. We're being challenged to go deeper, run farther, and operate in our gifts in far greater ways than ever before. Have fun with other believers and see how far He will take you.

> And let us consider how we may spur one another on toward love and good deeds, not giving up meeting together, as some are in the habit of doing, but encouraging one another—and all the more as you see the Day approaching (Hebrews 10:24–25).

Tool 4.1 Prayer for Healing from Fear

Pray the following prayer daily until you feel a release from fear in your life.

> *In the name of Jesus, I renounce the spirit of fear, and the related spirits of witchcraft and divination, and every way they have manifested in my life or my family line. I repent for not trusting You, Lord, and for all involvement with these evil spirits, and I command them to leave me now!*
>
> *Jesus, as it is written, I was not given a spirit of fear. But I admit that through the actions and behaviors of my ancestors and me, fear has entered my life and left marks on my DNA. I choose now to come into agreement with what Your word says. I was given a spirit of power, love, and self-control. I now choose according to Psalm 91:4 to accept and come under the protection of Your wings that is promised to me for the shelter from fear.*
>
> *I forgive _____ (name anyone the Holy Spirit brings to your mind) and I release them to the Lord.*
>
> *I repent for allowing the demonic spirit of fear to enter my life. I repent for my involvement in any and all actions that opened doors in my life and allowed the spirit of fear to enter. I choose now to no longer participate in the sins of my past. I am a new creation, and I am made new.*

I renounce the witchcraft spirit of fear in my life, and I command all fear present in my body, my DNA, my mind, and my heart to immediately fall off right now in Jesus' name.

I renounce manipulation, subjugation, and control used as a tool of the enemy to suppress my identity.

I renounce anxiety, enduring stress, and the feelings of punishment that manifest when fear is present.

I renounce all fruits of fear—lack of cognitive thought, elevated levels of cortisol and norepinephrine, high blood pressure, sleep disorders, suppressed immune system, high blood sugar, fatigue, and obesity.

I renounce the effect of fear on my mind, and I command my cerebral cortex to come alive, to begin operating with the mind of Christ. I renounce all mind-binding effects of fear on my mind. I am no longer blinded, susceptible, or easily deceived by demonic attacks of fear in my life.

I renounce bitterness toward God and an unhealthy fear of God. I renounce confusion and disgust with God or religion and loss of trust in God or Christian leaders. I renounce waiting on God to fix it, and I renounce despair due to the perceived loss of spirituality.

I declare that my cerebral cortex will no longer be bound by fear. I tell my mind to immediately reset and begin operating the way you were created. I declare restoration to my mind's ability to make decisions, to begin thinking at a higher level right now in the name of Jesus. Fear, you will not suppress my mind any longer—get off of me now!

I declare over my body complete physical restoration and healing from the unhealthy exposure to fear and its manifestations. Body, you will be healed, and all fear must leave me now!

I declare full restoration over my immune system—I command you to be strengthened and to begin operating at full strength, protecting me from all physical and demonic attacks.

I declare a full restoration of my endocrine system and I command my mood, growth functions, metabolism, and reproductive functions to be completely restored.

I declare and command a complete reversal of any and all damage caused by fear on my autonomic nervous system. I command all sleep disorders to cease and desist, and I bless my body with renewed vigor and restful sleep. I command all fatigue and low energy caused by fear to immediately be removed in the name of Jesus.

I declare and command that all effects of fear on my hypothalamus-pituitary-adrenal axis be removed and for my body to be realigned and reset according to how I was created.

I command all fear to immediately be removed from my DNA and for my DNA to begin immediately replicating with restored freedom.

I bless myself with a full and complete reset of my life. I declare that I am no longer a slave of fear!

Fear, where I am going you cannot follow. You are not my friend; you are not my comforter or my protector. I reject you and I break your hold on my life, and I now command you to leave my body now! Never to return. I now receive freedom from fear and torment from this moment forward, in Jesus' mighty name!

THE SCIENCE OF REJECTION

In Chapter 5 we learned how scientists have discovered rejection has damaging effects on the body. In this segment we equip you to begin healing from rejection so that your body can begin to heal as well.

Tool 5.1: Prayer to Renounce an Orphan Mindset and Release Sonship

The orphan mindset is one of the strongest roots of rejection that we all must deal with in order to heal. Our parents are meant to represent God's love to us. As humans, even the best parents will fail in some ways. Other parents will do quite the opposite of demonstrating God's love, instead causing fear, abuse, rejection, neglect, abandonment, and pain.

When those wounds are unhealed, it causes us to view God through the filter of how our earthly parents treated us. It negatively impacts our relationship with Him, making us feel that He is holding us at a distance due to our sin. It can also affect how we respond to other authority figures in our lives. It keeps us trapped in the orphan or slave mentality that we discussed in great detail in Chapter Five.

Blessings or Curses

Additionally, we know from scripture that there are blessings in honoring our parents: *"Honor your father and your mother, so that you may live long in the land the Lord your God is giving you"* (Exod. 20:12), and there are curses when we do not honor them: *"He will turn the hearts of the parents to their children, and the hearts of the children to their parents; or else I will come and strike the land with total destruction"* (Mal. 4:5-6).

Honoring Our Parents

Honoring does not mean that you must still obey your parents as an adult, or even that you must necessarily have a relationship with them, as that is not always possible or beneficial. It means having a heart attitude of honor toward them. It means treating them with kindness; forgiving them; refraining from harboring judgment, bitterness, anger, and hatred against them even though they might deserve it. It means praying for them with sincerity. It means asking God to align your thoughts and feelings about them with His.

Therefore, it is important to overcome the orphan mindset so that we can have healthy relationships with God and others and so that we will have blessings rather than curses on our lives. It is important because it is the only way we can grow in the Lord, glorify Him, and draw others to Him.

Read the signs of an orphan mentality, and ask the Holy Spirit to highlight any of these things that show up in you:

Signs of an Orphan Mentality

1. Unsubmissiveness, fear of submission, or fear of authority
2. Victim mentality
3. Striving and performing to gain approval and acceptance
4. Poor self-regulation
5. Being "reactive" rather than thinking and planning
6. Difficulty setting and accomplishing goals
7. Difficulty with delaying gratification and accepting "no" for an answer
8. Emotional immaturity and volatility—temper tantrums, sulking, pouting, shutting down, etc.
9. Extreme self-reliance: "I have to take care of myself" because "I can't depend on anyone else."
10. Getting in over your head and refusing to admit that or ask for help
11. Inappropriately exercising authority over others
12. Taking "justice" into your own hands, rather than going through proper channels to resolve disputes
13. Being needy or high-maintenance to get attention
14. Refusing to try something perceived as difficult, due to fear of failure

15. Wanting to maintain control of every situation in an attempt to feel secure and safe

16. Self-soothing and self-stimulating behaviors, such as OCD behaviors, substance abuse, addiction to food, sex, shopping, etc.

17. Living in a state of hyper-arousal, a constant state of heightened alertness and vigilance

18. Being proactively tough, aggressive, and dominant due to expecting a hostile environment

19. Behaving in a seductive or promiscuous way, in an attempt to feel in control of a situation

20. Entitlement attitude—the mindset that you are owed the same as whatever you see your neighbor get (regardless of whether you actually need it or have earned it)

21. Comparison, jealousy, and anger because you don't feel life is "fair"

22. Extreme attention seeking—trying to provoke a reaction and gain attention at any cost (even a negative reaction)

23. Being open and demonstrative with strangers while aloof and restrained with your own family

24. Always on the lookout for potentially new or better people to mentor you or fill your needs—better friends, a better spouse, a better boss, a better pastor or church; flitting from one person to the next, with no endurance or commitment in relationships

25. Having a paradigm of lack and competition

26. Hoarding

27. Hyper-competitiveness—making sure you get in line first, get the most, get "the best one"

28. Being jealous of someone else doing well, getting attention, or getting some coveted item, as though there is a finite amount of those things and "more for you equals less for me" (This can include jealousy over someone else getting a promotion, getting married, having a baby, or making a friend.)

29. Feelings of homelessness, never belonging, restlessness, and never being content or settled

30. Feelings of abandonment and rejection

Make some notes about what the Lord is telling you about yourself and keep those things in mind as you go through the following prayer.

Prayer to Renounce the Orphan Mindset and Release Sonship

Parents

Father God, I bring my relationship with my parents (or guardians) to You. I forgive them for failing to show me love the way You would have wanted and for every way that distorted my view of You. I forgive them for the times they were not kind, affectionate, understanding, or a safe place for me. Even though their actions were wrong, I choose to forgive them and release them to You, Lord.

I repent for the times I rebelled against my parents, for the times I judged them, and the times I dishonored them. I repent for the inner vow I made to reject their parenting and anything else they offered. Lord, please show me how this affected my relationship with You so that I can heal and embrace the sonship You offer.

Leadership and Authority

Regarding all other authority figures who have been in my life—pastors and church leadership, ministers, mentors, teachers, supervisors, and company leadership—I repent for the times I responded to them in rebellion, judgment, and dishonor. Going forward I want to always respond to those in authority according to Your leading, Lord. I no longer want to be reactionary based on my own wounding. I repent for being overly critical of leaders and using this as an excuse to stop listening to them. I choose to forgive all authority figures for every way they have hurt me. I forgive them for being unfair, dismissive, unkind, demeaning, manipulative, or not having time for me. I forgive the leaders who called themselves Christians but did not operate in love.

God

Lord, I repent for viewing You through the mindset of an orphan or slave. I repent for the times I responded to You in rebellion, judgment, anger, and dishonor. I repent for wanting to run my own life rather than yielding to You. You said in Your word that You accept me as a son or daughter, and I embrace that position now.

Renouncing Rebellion

I renounce and evict the spirit of rebellion I allowed to come into my life. I renounce all fear, manipulation and control, and extreme independence that attached to me due to the wounds I received from my parents and other authority figures. I break the curse off my life that was brought about by my dishonor of my parents and others in authority.

Ask the Lord to bring to your mind the time when you first embraced an orphan mindset. It may be a moment when you decided something like "I have to take care of myself," "I'm on my own," or "I won't listen to you anymore." That decision you made was an inner vow. Once the Lord has shown you, say, "I repent for and renounce the inner vow I made that _____, and I break the curse it brought on my life."

Embracing Sonship

Lord, I invite You to bring my beliefs and emotions into alignment with who You are (a loving and perfect Father) and who You say I am (a beloved and accepted son or daughter). I invite You to change the way I view and relate to authority figures so that I will respond to them according to Your discernment and Your leading. I ask You to restore anything I lost (opportunities, financial blessings, relational connections) due to being in rebellion. I receive You as my Father, and I thank You for making me Your child!

Tool 5.2: Identifying Roots of Rejection

Before breaking off the spirit of rejection, it can be helpful to have insight as to how it got a foothold in the first place. Read through this list of common entry points and mark the ones that pertain to you or your family line. Add to the list anything else that comes to mind. If a painful memory suddenly surfaces and you feel it is hindering you from moving forward in the process, use Tool 9.1: Inner Healing Method to process that memory before continuing.

Common Entry Points of Rejection

1. Being an unplanned pregnancy about which your family was not happy

2. Being a girl when your family wanted a boy, or vice versa

3. Trauma during the time your mother was pregnant with you or during your birth

4. Being separated from your mother directly after birth

5. Being given up for adoption or the threat of being given up for adoption

Regarding the four items above, the baby can sense fear in the mother's emotions, and is very cognizant of any separation from the mother (the only home the baby has ever known up to that point). Not knowing how to interpret these circumstances and emotions, the baby may internalize them as rejection.

6. Feeling you don't meet expectations or are below average in some area—talent, looks, achievements, athletic skill, academics, personality, etc.

7. Feeling you are a burden to others

8. Feeling disconnected in important relationships (parents, spouses, immediate family)

9. Feeling guilt or shame over your mistakes and sins

10. Feeling guilt or shame that others have piled on you, even when you were not at fault

11. Being abused physically, sexually, or verbally (including being "bullied")

12. Being neglected or abandoned

13. Being consistently treated with a harsh, angry, frustrated, or cold manner

14. Being fired, laid off, or demoted

15. Being rejected for promotions or new positions

16. An unfaithful spouse or romantic partner

17. Divorce, broken engagement, or breakup

18. Betrayal/backstabbing

19. Any number of events that we may have misinterpreted, especially while we were babies or children, such as being taken away from your mother for an extended time directly after birth due to an emergency or other situation

Tool 5.3: Prayer of Healing from Rejection

Father, I invite and release Your healing into my body, soul, and spirit.

In the name of Jesus, I renounce the spirit of rejection and the related spirits of jealousy and haughtiness and every way they have manifested in my life or my family line. I repent for all involvement with these evil spirits, and I tell them to leave me now!

I speak to every part of my body and soul that has been shut down, suppressed, or impaired, that has not been performing at normal levels, and I command you to function in fullness, normalcy, and ease.

I speak to every part of my body and soul that suffered effects of physical abuse, verbal abuse, sexual abuse, emotional abuse, substance abuse, self-abuse, or neglect, and I release God's love into you and command you to be healed now.

I speak to every part of my body that has been out of balance—blood counts, cell counts, hormones, blood sugar, blood pressure, heart rate, bone marrow, skeletal structure, or anything else—and I command you to come into optimum balance.

I speak to every part of my body that has been neglected or not receiving what it needs to thrive. Lord, I ask for wisdom and revelation to provide what my body needs in the physical, emotional, and spiritual realms, and I tell every part of my body—you are important, needed, loved, and accepted as you are. I command every system of my body to come into perfect communication and alignment so that every part receives what it needs to thrive.

I speak to every part of my body and soul that has been weighed down with burdens, lies I've believed, and false responsibilities; every part that has felt weighed down, strangled out, wasted away, and I speak new life into you. I renounce perfectionism. I renounce setting a standard for myself that I must reach in order to be worthy of love. I release myself from all judgments made against me based on my physical appearance or for any other perceived shortcoming, by me and others. I release all anger at myself for not being good enough or not doing well enough. I am grateful for my body, for how hard it fights to protect me and all the functions it carries out each day. I accept myself as I am, because God accepts me as I am. And while I commit to being a better steward of my body, I also declare that I am both a "work of art" and a "work in progress" at the same time. Instead of self-punishment, I will make steps toward health inspired by love.

I command all chronic inflammation to be healed. I speak to results of self-hatred and self-rejection and tell all autoimmune disorders, anything that would cause my body to attack itself, and all eating disorders to halt immediately. I accept and release into my body and soul the healing power of Jesus, His love and acceptance to set everything right again.

I declare a new era in my relationships, a new grace on me to make meaningful friendships and maintain them, new discernment to choose friendships that are godly and life giving. I trust You, Holy Spirit, to align me with the right body of believers so that I can grow and contribute in an environment that is biblically grounded, spiritually healthy, and emotionally mature.

I declare that I am a child of God, that I was created by Him because He wanted me. I believe what God says about me—that I am wanted, accepted, valued, respected, included, cared for, and loved.

Father God, I thank You and praise You that my healing has already begun and that You will carry it to completion!

TOOLS FROM CHAPTER 6

NEUROSCIENCE AND YOUR THOUGHT LIFE

In this segment we will equip you to release healing into the neural pathways and regions of your brain.

Tool 6.1: Renewing the Mind

In this segment we will equip you to identify lies you have believed and toxic thoughts that have caused damage to your physical brain. You will also learn how to uproot and replace them with God's word! When you flood your brain with healthy thoughts, physical healing will occur.

Identifying Toxic Thoughts

Begin by identifying toxic thoughts, also known as lies you have believed or ungodly beliefs. These are thoughts you have that do not agree with God's word. Ask the Holy Spirit to bring them to your mind. Here are just a few examples:

- I am ugly, unattractive, undesirable, people don't like me.
- I am a slow learner, I have a poor memory, I make bad decisions.
- I am dirty, damaged, broken.
- Things will never get better.
- I will never be good enough no matter how hard I try.
- God is angry and/or disappointed with me.
- I cannot not trust anyone because they will let me down.
- I will never be able to accomplish my goals or dreams.

Get a piece of notebook paper and draw a line down the center from top to bottom. On the left side write "Toxic Thoughts" at the top, and underneath write down every one of your toxic thoughts that you identified in this exercise. Keep the paper as we will use it for the next step.

Finding the Truth According to God

On the right side of your paper, at the top write down "Blessings of Truth." Underneath that, you are going to write the truth that counters every single lie you wrote down on the left. This may take some time, but it is *important*. You will need to get quiet and ask the Holy Spirit to give you statements of truth. You will need to search scriptures that relate to your topic. Turn those scriptures into statements about yourself. Here is an example of what your list might look like:

TOXIC THOUGHTS	BLESSINGS OF TRUTH
God is angry with me.	God does not look upon me in anger; He is gracious with me (Jer. 3:12). His anger is turned away, and He comforts me (Isa. 12:1).
I am stupid.	I have the mind of Christ (1 Cor. 2:16). I am filled with the Holy Spirit, and He will provide wisdom, understanding, and knowledge for the tasks He has given me (Exod. 35:31).
If people really get to know me, then they won't like me.	God designed me for a purpose, and there are people who need what He put in me. As I allow myself to be the unique person God designed, I will attract godly and fulfilling friendships.

Daily Blessings of Truth

Once your list is complete, cut it in half along the center, vertical line. The two columns will now be separated into two pieces of paper.

Take the "Toxic Thoughts" list and say out loud: "I repent for believing the following lies, and I now break agreement with them! I renounce the lies that (and here you read out loud everything you wrote down)." Then destroy that list of toxic thoughts! Tear it into pieces, stomp on it, and throw it away! This is a prophetic act demonstrating the Lord destroying the works of the enemy in your life.

Take the "Blessings of Truth" list and put it on your bathroom mirror or somewhere you will see it every day. Every single day, for at least 60 days, read the blessings over yourself out loud. Say:

In the name of Jesus I come into agreement with the word of God! I declare and receive the following blessings, and believe they will all come to fruition in my life (and here you read out loud all of the blessings of truth you wrote down).

Ask the Holy Spirit to increase your faith and help you to truly believe these statements in your heart.

While we recommend at least 60 days, continue to do this for as long as you need to. It is so life giving that it may become a daily habit that you continue indefinitely! You can add more blessings as you go.

Tool 6.2: Prayer to Release Healing from Toxic Thoughts

Pray these words aloud to release healing from all damage that was caused by toxic thinking:

In the name of Jesus, I invite and release God's healing over my brain.

I renounce the spirits of lying, error, deaf and dumb, slumber and unbelief, and bondage (that commonly attach to the brain) and every way they have manifested in my life or my family line. I repent for all involvement with these evil spirits, and I command them to leave me now!

I evict from my brain all anxiety, depression, negativity, sleep disorders, eating disorders, hostility, and suicidal thoughts.

I command healing and rewiring of my neural pathways, and I tell all inflammation in them to dissipate.

I declare healing over all damage that toxic thoughts or trauma caused to my heart, my blood pressure, my circulation and blood vessels, or my immune system. I declare healing over every single part of my body that was damaged by toxic thinking or trauma.

I tell my brain to have full cognition, cognitive flexibility, and to operate at full capacity.

I bless myself with an increase in creative thinking and problem solving.

I command my brain to process at full speed as it was designed to do.

I command perfect function, growth, and development of my pre-frontal cortex, my cerebellum, and every lobe, cortex, and region of my brain.

I bless my brain to have excellent focus, clarity of thought, and attention span.

I command my brain to have proper processing of and control over my emotions.

I bless myself with excellent metacognition (being aware of my own thoughts).

I tell my cortisol levels to drop to healthy levels, and my serotonin to increase to healthy levels.

I bless myself to have a positive outlook that is based in reality as seen through God's eyes.

Thank You, Father, for healing me and putting everything right!

Tool 6.3: Meditation Method

The following meditation method will be a guide as you enter into deeper mindfulness and relationship with the Holy Spirit. Follow these instructions as you learn, then over time allow the Holy Spirit to further guide you into your personal meditative process.

True biblical meditation is not designed to empty the mind. Rather, it is designed to enhance your existing relationship with the Holy Spirit. Allow the Holy Spirit to engage with your thoughts and bring clarity to items that may have been pushed aside.

"Be still, and know that I am God" (Ps. 46:10). This scripture exemplifies the need to be at rest and meditate with Him. Two of the key words in this passage are *still* and *know*. *Still* is the Hebrew word *raphah*, meaning "to cease activities and to be idle." *Know* is the Hebrew work *yada*, meaning "to ascertain by seeing, using a variety of senses."

Our thoughts are not dangerous or scary but when suppressed can become toxic, eventually becoming unresolved and unpacified emotions. Toxic thoughts and emotions have an adverse effect, not only on our minds but on our physical bodies as well. Biblical meditation will refocus your mind, will, and emotions on what is true, restoring peace.

Start by getting into a comfortable posture. Use a comfortable chair or couch with pillows that you can fall into. Perhaps a soft rug with pillows to surround you. Just be comfortable and at rest. Try to avoid a position that requires adjustment or shifting.

Begin with the following prayer:

Holy Spirit, You are welcome here, I present myself to You for meditation. I instruct my mind and thoughts to focus on You. I speak protection over my mind and declare that my mind, will, and emotions are open to the guidance of the Holy Spirit.

I cancel every assignment of the enemy over my mind, will, and emotions. I bind every demonic entity in this room from interacting with me and I tell you to go from this place. I thank You, Jesus, for Your protection and give myself completely to You. Have Your way.

Proceed to the next page and through the following meditation stages of breathing, focus, rest, peace, thoughtfulness, and finally Holy Spirit guidance.

1. Close your eyes and begin to breathe deeply (repeat three to six times).
   a. Fast inward breath through the nose
   b. Slow exhale through the mouth (like blowing up a balloon)
   c. Mentally take note of the sounds, smells, and senses in your environment. This will help you become focused and present with the Holy Spirit.

2. Remain at peace and allow your mind to wander; remember, you gave the Holy Spirit permission to take you where you need.

3. Allow your thoughts to come and go unhindered.

   a. Engage the Holy Spirit in mental conversation concerning any of these thoughts.

   b. Limit any verbal speaking to concepts that aid in your focus and meditation.

   c. You have no obligation to speak; sometimes rest is best, allowing the Holy Spirit to guide your thoughts.

   d. Remember, meditation is not prayer, but mindful focus of thoughts and listening (see Phil. 4:8).

4. Allow the Holy Spirit time to respond and speak to your heart and mind.

5. Continue regular breathing and remain at peace as long as you desire.

6. After a comfortable time of peaceful rest ask the Holy Spirit:

   a. What do You want to tell me today?

   b. What is my next step toward what You are showing me?

   c. Any question you desire that might engage the Holy Spirit in your life.

7. Remain in this peaceful moment and simply listen to the Holy Spirit if He is speaking.

   a. If the Holy Spirit is silent, it's OK. That means you simply need to rest at peace in meditation.

8. Open your eyes when you feel the meditation has completed—usually 10 to 15 minutes in the beginning, gradually increasing your time as desired.

GUT, BRAIN, AND HEART

In this segment we equip you to begin emotional and spiritual healing as it relates to your heart and your gut. In Chapter Seven we learned that scientists believe the heart (not the brain) is the seat of emotional intelligence, and the gut has a type of neural network that plays into making decisions based on feeling rather than logic. Here we take you through several processes that remove spiritual and emotional roadblocks to physical healing.

Tool 7.1: Breaking Inner Vows

We learned from scripture that the heart is where we make vows.

An inner vow is a resolution you make in your heart, usually involving the idea that you will "never" or you will "always" do something. We say or think things like "I will never be like my parents!" or "I will always be a loner." Inner vows usually stem from points of pain, and are meant to protect ourselves against, or brace ourselves against, further pain. They also stem from judgments we make against others. In the example, "I will never be like my parents!" we are making a judgment against our parents that there is nothing about them worth learning from or emulating, that there is nothing good in them. Now it may be true that over-all they are not a good choice of someone to emulate. However, the result of such an inner vow is the exact opposite of what we desire. A person who vows never to become like their parents has set themselves up to become exactly like their parents, because they are in sin by holding that judgment (only God is qualified to judge a person's heart), and that sin opens the door for the same spirits to operate in their own life. Instead of saying "I will never be like my parents," we should identify the opposite and declare that over ourselves: "I will be a kind and understanding person." We should also forgive our parents. Furthermore, when we make inner vows we are trusting in our own rules to keep us safe or on track, instead of trusting in the Holy Spirit.

Prayer to Break Inner Vows

Get quiet and ask the Holy Spirit to bring to mind all inner vows you have made. If there are multiple vows, then make a list of them. Then address each, one at a time, with the following prayer:

1. In the name of Jesus, I repent for and renounce the inner vow where I said in my heart: _____ (speak out the inner vow you made). I break this vow now in Jesus' name!

2. I repent for and break all judgments I made against _____ (list the people you judged).

3. I forgive anyone who hurt me in such a way that it influenced me to make this vow. In particular I forgive _____ .

4. I replace that inner vow with reliance and trust in You, Holy Spirit. I trust You to protect me, to keep me on track, and to guide me in all things. I trust You to give me positive goals for myself based on emulating Jesus and based on who You have called me to be. Amen!

Tool 7.2: Breaking Ungodly Soul Ties
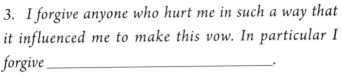

As we learned, the heart is highly involved in emotional intelligence, but it can be hindered when damaged by negative emotions. Soul ties are one source of chronic negative emotions.

A soul tie is a strong emotional connection forged between the hearts of two people. It can also be between a person and a place, animal, or thing.

When you have a soul tie with another person, it is like an invisible cord that keeps you tied to that person, no matter how far apart you are. It means you may sense their emotions, their struggles, their joy, or their distress from a thousand miles away, and vice versa.

God designed soul ties to bond people together in healthy ways. Marriage is an obvious example, as sexual contact was designed by God to form a healthy soul tie between a husband and wife:

> *"For this reason a man will leave his father and mother and be united to his wife, and the two will become one*

*flesh." So they are no longer two, but one flesh. Therefore
what God has joined together, let no one separate* (Mark
10:7–9).

The Greek word translated *united* means "being glued
together, stuck together, or joined with closely" (Strong's #G4347,
proskollaō, pronounced pros-kol-lah'-o).

Another biblical example is the close friendship between King
David and Jonathan:

> *And it came to pass, when he had made an end of speak-
> ing unto Saul, that the soul of Jonathan was knit with the
> soul of David, and Jonathan loved him as his own soul*
> (1 Samuel 18:1 KJV).

The Hebrew word translated *knit* means "to tie, physically
(gird, confine, compact) or mentally (in love, league)" (Strong's
#H7194, *qāšar*, pronounced kaw-shar').

When two people have a *godly* soul tie, the connection
draws them both closer to God as well as to one another. It is
a connection of encouragement, support, accountability, honesty, and love. It is iron sharpening iron. It will bear fruit of
each person growing in the Lord and spurring one another on
in the work God has called them to. Godly soul ties are forged
through God's leading and through mutual love of Him and
each other.

Ungodly soul ties are forged through sin. Sexual contact outside of marriage, whether or not it went as far as intercourse, and
whether consensual or through being sinned against via sexual
assault, will result in an ungodly soul tie. This includes fornication

(even if the man and woman later get married to each other) and adultery. As we read above, sexual contact effectively glues two people together. Think about gluing two pieces of paper together and letting them dry. If you then pull them apart, they will not separate cleanly; each will have rips and tears and pieces of the other paper left stuck to it. This is a picture of what happens to people. The relationship may have ended, but each person is left with damage and with residue from the other person stuck to their soul. This is why even a divorced person should break soul ties with their ex-spouse, because the connection that was once sanctified through marriage is no longer right or proper to have in place in context of a broken covenant.

Ungodly soul ties can also be made through lust, abuse, trauma, fear, and co-dependency. *An ungodly soul tie is one that hooks your mind, your will, or your emotions and pulls you away from God.* It might bring confusion, distraction, fear, shame, procrastination, or hindrances in following God's will for your life. It might bring toxic thoughts or sinful thoughts or behaviors.

A person might have an ungodly soul tie with a *place* when they feel such a pull to it that they can never be happy or content living anywhere else. Or if they find their sense of pride and value based on where they are from.

A person might have a soul tie with an *animal* when the animal becomes their primary source of comfort, purpose, friendship, or value, above God.

They might have a soul tie with an *object* when they revere it or can't bear the thought of losing it, almost as though it were a living thing.

This is why it is important to break all ungodly soul ties so that we can move forward serving God in freedom!

Prayer to Break Ungodly Soul Ties

> Father, in the name of Jesus, I ask You to reveal every ungodly soul tie in my life so that it can be undone. I want all hindrances to my relationship with You to be removed!
>
> 1. I break all soul ties forged through consensual sexual contact outside of marriage with _____ (list the names, and if there are any you don't know or don't remember then list a description such as "the woman I met at the party"). I forgive these people for their part in this sin, and I forgive myself and accept God's forgiveness for my part in this sin. From this point forward I present my body as a living sacrifice to You, Lord. I turn away from sexual sin and reserve the sexual use of my body for marriage according to Your command and Your design.
>
> 2. I break all soul ties that were forced upon me through sexual assault, molestation, or rape committed by _____ (list the names, and if there are any you don't know or don't remember then list a description such as "the boy who lived down the street"). I forgive these people for sinning against me, for inflicting trauma and damage on my body and soul, and for the feelings of fear, confusion, uncleanness, shame, guilt, and grief they caused.

3. *I agree that by the blood of Jesus I am cleansed of all unrighteousness, that my body is pure and acceptable and whole!*

4. *I break all ungodly soul ties with ex-spouses, including* _____ *(list their names). I forgive them for their part in breaking our marriage covenant, and I forgive myself and accept God's forgiveness for my part in breaking our marriage covenant.*

5. *I break all nonsexual, ungodly soul ties with other people, including* _____ *(list anyone who comes to mind; these ties may be due to things like trauma, abuse, lust, fear, or co-dependency). I forgive those who brought about such ties by sinning against me in any way, and I forgive myself and accept God's forgiveness for all such ties that were forged through my own sin. I submit myself to You, Lord, and ask for Your help as I choose to turn away from every sinful thought pattern and behavior.*

6. *I break all ungodly soul ties with any animal, place, or object* _____ *(list anything that comes to mind). I repent for this unnatural and ungodly connection. I forgive myself, and I accept God's forgiveness.*

7. *By the authority of Jesus who said whatever we loose on earth will be loosed in heaven (Matt. 18:18-19), I hereby break every ungodly soul tie that connects me to any person, place, or thing! Lord, I ask You to sever those ties now, in Jesus' name.*

8.   *I command my body, soul, and spirit to forget every ungodly union. I tell my emotions to let go and forget those unions.*

9.   *I command the shattered pieces of my soul to reunite with me. I command all residue from others to detach from my soul and return to them.*

10. *Thank You, Father God, for healing and restoring me by Your love and power! Amen!*

Tool 7.3: Prayer to Release Healing of the Heart and Gut

In the name of Jesus, I renounce the spirits of heaviness and depression, fear, perversity and whoredoms, anger and bitterness (that commonly attach to the heart and gut) and every way they have manifested in my life or my family line. I repent for all involvement with these evil spirits and command them to leave me now!

In accordance with God's word, I command healing into the neurons of my brain, heart, and gut. I tell the "three brains" of my body to work together in harmony so that I can effectively manage my emotions and be in perfect health. I speak healing over my cellular memory, including my epigenetic memory, DNA memory, RNA memory, and protein memory.

I release healing into my enteric nervous system and my autonomic nervous system. I command all communication between neurons in my brain, heart, and gut be in perfect order, alignment, and function. I speak healing over my vagus nerve and my gut-brain axis.

I release healing into the neurons of my digestive system. I command my gut microbiome to come into perfect balance and function. I release healing over every area that may have been damaged through imbalance or dysfunction in my gut or by suppressed emotions, including my emotions, my immune system, my cells, my blood, my brain, my personality, or any other part of my being.

I release healing into the neurons in my heart. I tell my "heart's brain" and my entire heart organ to be healed from all effects of trauma, emotional pain, heartbreak, extreme grief, and to be restored. I command regular, smooth, harmonious heart rhythms, perfect blood pressure, perfect heart rate, health, and normal function of all valves, veins, arteries, and electrical signals.

I command my heart to correctly play its part in aligning various systems in my body so that they can function in harmony.

I command my heart to correctly interpret emotional context and accurately send that information to my brain via neurological, biochemical, biophysical, and energetic communications.

I bless myself with an increase in emotional intelligence. Lord, Your word says, "A cheerful heart is good medicine, but a crushed spirit dries up the bones" (Proverbs 17:22).

I ask for Your help as I choose to move forward with a cheerful heart. I thank You for healing my physical body and my emotions. Amen!

THE SCIENCE OF FORGIVENESS

Forgiveness is the first part of deliverance ministry. Releasing unforgiveness removes any foothold the enemy has, allowing him to remain and torment. After releasing forgiveness, you are ready to begin removing every demonic attachment in your life.

We begin with forgiveness because we are commanded by God in Leviticus 19:18:

> Do not seek revenge or bear a grudge against anyone…
> but love your neighbor as yourself. I am the Lord.

Then in Matthew 18:21–35 we read the story of the master forgiving the debtor's debt. But the debtor did not pass down his blessing. As a result of his unforgiveness, he was given to his tormentors:

> In anger his master handed him over to the jailers to be tortured, until he should pay back all he owed (Matthew 18:34).

Tool 8.1: Forgiveness Healing Method

Begin with a prayer to invite the Holy Spirit into the room.

> *Holy Spirit, I invite You into this room, into my heart, and into my mind. I no longer wish to hold any unforgiveness in my life. I declare unforgiveness in my life to be trespassing on my freedom. Right now, I choose to address and release any issues of unforgiveness that I am holding on to. Holy Spirit, would You reveal to me anyone I need to forgive?*

Pause for a brief moment and feel the weighty presence of the glory of the Lord come into the room.

Note for the minister if present:

Instruct the client, "Please let me know when the Holy Spirit begins showing you names and faces." It is common for the Holy Spirit to reveal a list of people whom you will need to forgive. This is not the rule, however; if the Holy Spirit only reveals one name to you, then that's your assignment this time.

- Begin with the person the Holy Spirit reveals.
- Picture this person sitting directly in front of you. Note: We are not reliving the memory. We are simply looking at the person's face.
- Tell the person exactly what they did and how they hurt you. Do not justify. Be real, be raw, don't feel the need to use proper Christian language. For example: "You failed me as a friend; you were not

there when I needed you; you were a horrible, terrible person to me."

- Tell the person, "What you did was not OK, you hurt me, but I choose to forgive you and I release you to the Lord."
  - Immediately transition your thoughts to intentionally think of something you adore and that brings you joy (unrelated to the wound).
  - This will begin to train the mind to release the pain of the event and allow forgiveness to set in.
- Move to the next person on the list and repeat the process, every time ending with something that brings you joy. This process is biblically grounded in Philippians 4:9, "think on these things" to renew the mind.

TOOLS FROM CHAPTER 9

INNER HEALING

In this segment we will equip you to partner with the Lord for healing of your memories and emotions.

Tool 9.1: Inner Healing Method

Begin with the following prayer:

Lord, I invite You to take me to any memory or moment of trauma in my life that You want to heal in me. I bind all distracting spirits and give permission to You, Lord, to have Your way. I desire to hear from You, Lord, and I seek healing from all wounds and trauma in my past.

1. Close your eyes. Keep them closed throughout the memory.

2. Ask the Lord: "Lord, take me to a memory that You would like to heal." Quietly allow the Lord to bring you to a memory in your history.

3. While you are in the memory, look into the eyes of the person(s) who hurt you. There may be several people; you will address them each individually.

4. Speak to them directly and tell them exactly how they make you feel in this moment. Be brutally honest—don't justify their actions or make excuses for them.

5. Tell them: "What you did was wrong, it was not OK, and it will never be OK."
   a. Now forgive them: "But I choose to forgive you, and I release you to the Lord."
   b. Do this for everyone in the memory who has hurt you.

6. Ask the Lord: "Is there anyone else I need to forgive?"
   a. Do you need to forgive yourself for any involvement in this memory?
   b. If so: "I forgive myself for _____."

7. Are you harboring any negative emotions, thoughts, or unforgiveness against the Lord?
   a. If so: "I forgive You, Lord, for _____."

8. Invite the Holy Spirit into the ministry room. You should expect to sense the glory of the Holy Spirit come into the room.

9. If you are having trouble sensing the presence of the Holy Spirit:

    a. Say: "Lord, is there anyone else I need to forgive?"

    b. Bind all distracting spirits: "I bind all distractions preventing me from seeing the Lord."

10. Once the Lord's presence is felt in the room, ask Him the following questions:

    a. Ask: "What lie did I believe?"

    b. Ask: "What is the truth?" Allow Him to reveal and speak truth to you.

    c. Ask: "Did any demon attach to me?"

    d. Ask: "Will You remove the demonic spirit that attached to me?"

11. Allow the Lord to minister to you. You are not in a hurry, just let Him work and watch what He does.

12. Stay in this peaceful glory moment until He is done and you feel peace in that memory and all pain of the moment is erased.

13. Ask the Lord: "Is there another memory that You would like to heal?"

14. If so, start over. If He does not take you to another memory, rest in the assurance that you are free!

How to Receive and Minister Freedom

Tool 10.1: Practical Steps to Maintain Freedom

When you receive freedom, the enemy does not like it! He will try to regain what he considers his territory. But never fear! Before, when he was in your house and had you cornered, it was a difficult fight. Now, the situation has drastically changed! He has been kicked out and locked outside. You may hear him trying the door handle, but as long as you keep the door closed and locked he cannot regain entrance into your life.

Also remember that God is your Father, He is infinitely stronger than the enemy, and He will help you!

Here are practical steps you can take to keep your doors shut and locked to the enemy.

Rest in God. Spend time simply enjoying His presence!

Pray, meditate, worship, read the Bible with no agenda other than to spend time with the Lord. Practice hearing God's voice; be still and listen for Him. Ask Him to help you *feel* and *receive* His love; when this happens, it transforms you from the inside out!

Make a habit of seeking the Lord's guidance.

As humans, we tend to go as far as we can on our own power before asking for help. However, God did not design us to walk through life alone. We need only to look at Isaiah 2:3 where it is written:

> *Many peoples will come and say, "Come, let us go up to the mountain of the Lord, to the temple of the God of Jacob. He will teach us his ways, so that we may walk in his paths."*

We are meant to climb the mountain with Him, receive teaching from Him, and walk His paths together. If you need help, you need only to seek the face of Jesus.

Do life with a community of believers.

Having regular fellowship with other believers is crucial to maintaining your freedom. This does not necessarily need to be a formal "church" that has its own building and a seminary graduate holding the office of pastor. Rather, it can be a Bible study, a home group, a men's or women's study group, a group of friends with whom you meet to pray and worship, etc.

We all need others in our day-to-day lives who will pray for us, encourage us, and sharpen us as iron sharpens iron, because

God Himself designed us to function this way. We are also commanded to use our spiritual gifts and talents to serve others in
the body of Christ. To say that we don't need this or that we can
manage on our own *by any rationale* is to *deny God's design* and *dis-
obey His commands!*

Here are just a *few* scriptures on the importance of
biblical community:

> *Carry each other's burdens, and in this way you will ful-
> fill the law of Christ* (Galatians 6:2).
>
> *Therefore confess your sins to each other and pray for
> each other so that you may be healed. The prayer of a
> righteous person is powerful and effective* (James 5:16).
>
> *As iron sharpens iron, so one person sharpens another*
> (Proverbs 27:17).
>
> *For where two or three gather in my name, there am I
> with them* (Matthew 18:20).
>
> *So in Christ we, though many, form one body, and each
> member belongs to all the others* (Romans 12:5).
>
> *Live in harmony with one another. Do not be proud, but
> be willing to associate with people of low position. Do not
> be conceited* (Romans 12:16).
>
> *I long to see you so that I may impart to you some spiri-
> tual gift to make you strong—that is, that you and I may
> be mutually encouraged by each other's faith* (Romans
> 1:11-12).
>
> *And let us consider how we may spur one another on
> toward love and good deeds, not giving up meeting*

together, as some are in the habit of doing, but encouraging one another—and all the more as you see the Day approaching (Hebrews 10:24-25).

So that there should be no division in the body, but that its parts should have equal concern for each other. If one part suffers, every part suffers with it; if one part is honored, every part rejoices with it. Now you are the body of Christ, and each one of you is a part of it (1 Corinthians 12:25-27).

Each of you should use whatever gift you have received to serve others, as faithful stewards of God's grace in its various forms (1 Peter 4:10).

Two are better than one, because they have a good return for their labor: If either of them falls down, one can help the other up. But pity anyone who falls and has no one to help them up. Also, if two lie down together, they will keep warm. But how can one keep warm alone? Though one may be overpowered, two can defend themselves. A cord of three strands is not quickly broken (Ecclesiastes 4:9-12).

We often have people who are not in community tell us, "All I need is Jesus." That is true regarding salvation. However, Jesus Himself is the one who commands us to be in community and who designed us to need one another for proper spiritual growth. Being on your own makes you weak and vulnerable—an easy target for a prowling lion. Being in relationship with others helps you maintain perspective and keep your blind spots covered. It affords you prayer cover and life-giving encouragement. It also brings a need for grace, understanding, forgiveness, humbleness, generosity, selflessness, consideration, kindness, conflict resolution, and honesty tempered by love. God uses all of this to shape us more into His likeness. Additionally, our spiritual gifts were not designed to work in a vacuum, but we are each given pieces of a puzzle (see 1 Cor. 13:9). When we work as a team, we put more pieces together and see more of the whole. If you are attempting to minister to others but you are going it alone, then you are out of alignment with God's design. If you do not currently have biblical community, then begin searching earnestly and ask God to lead you to the right place. He will be faithful to do so!

Go through deliverance with a reputable ministry.

There is much value in receiving ministry through a trained and anointed team who can see past your blind spots and pool their spiritual gifts together to create an environment of respectful, effective ministry.

Make forgiveness a habit.

Where there is forgiveness there is freedom. Demonic spirits enjoy preying on those who refuse to forgive. Unforgiveness is like having footholds in our life that demonic spirits such as fear can hold on to. Forgiveness removes those footholds and closes the door to every stronghold.

> *Be kind and compassionate to one another, forgiving each other, just as in Christ God forgave you* (Ephesians 4:32).

Make inner healing a habit.

As you go through life, people will hurt you occasionally. Practice first aid for your emotional wounds by going through inner healing as often as needed.

Make gratitude a habit (see Eph. 4:32, Col. 3:15).

God tells us to be grateful, and it has an amazing healing impact on our bodies!

> *Let the peace of Christ rule in your hearts, since as members of one body you were called to peace. And be thankful (Colossians 3:15).*

Make meditation a habit.

Biblical meditation is part of God's design for us to commune with Him! It also has healing effects on our bodies. Meditation is a great time to incorporate the gratitude mentioned above.

Make renewing the mind a habit.

- Read the Bible often.
- Read your list of blessings out loud over yourself daily.
- Practice free journaling—take five minutes a day to write down all thoughts running through your head, whatever they may be, with no filter. You can throw the page away when you are done. The point is to develop awareness of what you are thinking and identify toxic thoughts that need to be brought to the Lord for truth and healing.

- Feed your mind according to Philippians 4:4–9! Consider your books, music, entertainment, etc. and whether they meet the criteria:

Rejoice in the Lord always. I will say it again: Rejoice! Let your gentleness be evident to all. The Lord is near. Do not be anxious about anything, but in every situation, by prayer and petition, with thanksgiving, present your requests to God. And the peace of God, which transcends all understanding, will guard your hearts and your minds in Christ Jesus.

Finally, brothers and sisters, whatever is true, whatever is noble, whatever is right, whatever is pure, whatever is lovely, whatever is admirable—if anything is excellent or praiseworthy—think about such things. Whatever you have learned or received or heard from me, or seen in me—put it into practice. And the God of peace will be with you.

- Take control over your thoughts; deny the demonic attempt to infiltrate your life by way of your mind. Here is a simple outline that will get you started on the right trajectory:
  - Worship the Lord (rejoice).
  - Practice gentleness.
  - Pray continually and practice thankfulness.
  - Guard your thought life so that it will glorify God.

- Continue to practice all of these things, and the God of peace (spirit of peace) will be with you.

Deny entrance to fear.

Understand that you were not given a spirit of fear by God. Therefore, any chronic fear in your life comes through demonic influence. Declare the following scriptures, deny the spirit of fear any ground in your life, and walk in freedom. Bless yourself continuously with power, love, and self-control. As you bless yourself, you are changing your DNA—literally, resetting in yourself the ability to be powerful and confident.

> For the Spirit God gave us does not make us timid [fearful], but gives us power, love and self-discipline (2 Timothy 1:7).

Receive peace and sheltering:

> He will cover you with his feathers, and under his wings you will find refuge; his faithfulness will be your shield and rampart. You will not fear the terror of night, nor the arrow that flies by day (Psalm 91:4–5).

The battle is sometimes waged while we rest and submit our fears to God. He fights for you, He wins for you, and He will never leave you:

> Be strong and courageous. Do not be afraid or terrified because of them, for the Lord your God goes with you; he will never leave you nor forsake you (Deuteronomy 31:6).

The Lord is my light and my salvation—whom shall I fear? The Lord is the stronghold of my life—of whom shall I be afraid? When the wicked advance against me to devour me, it is my enemies and my foes who will stumble and fall. Though an army besiege me, my heart will not fear; though war break out against me, even then I will be confident (Psalm 27:1–3).

I will glory in the Lord; let the afflicted hear and rejoice. Glorify the Lord with me; let us exalt his name together. I sought the Lord, and he answered me; he delivered me from all my fears (Psalm 34:2–4).

Walk in righteousness.

Having turned away from sin, don't go back! Yes, we all sin occasionally, and we must repent and accept forgiveness. It is when we choose to adopt a pattern of sinful behavior in our lives that it opens the door for the enemy to come back in. Choose instead to walk in righteousness as an expression of your love for God, and the enemy won't stand a chance!

ACKNOWLEDGMENTS

Looking back over this process we have such thankful hearts for those who selflessly helped us along the way. We specifically want to thank Greg and Rebecca Greenwood who encouraged us to turn our teachings into a book.

Thank you to Becca Greenwood for writing the foreword, and Doris Wagner for writing the introduction; we are beyond honored to have their support.

Thank you to Joyce Nicodin, Charissa Goossen, and Giselle Goossen, who swooped in like the calvary to watch our small children for many hours as deadlines approached, while believing in us and cheering us on.

Thank you to Kara Puckett for taking more than her share of the load in leading deliverance sessions with our ministry, which freed up more hours of precious writing time.

Thank you to Tina Pugh and everyone at Destiny Image for their excellence and encouragement during this process, including Eileen Rockwell and her team for the beautiful cover design.

About Jareb and Petra Nott

Jareb and Petra Nott are co-founders of Engage Deliverance & Training. Over the last decade, they have operated both in deliverance ministery and as biblical teachers. Their goal is to equip churches and ministries across the nation with deliverance ministry tools and training for setting captives free. They have spoken and led classes at numerous venues and churches, including serving as leaders and teachers at Christian Harvest Training Center, an apostolic center founded and led by Becca and Greg Greenwood. Married 23 years, they live in Colorado with their three children. Connect with them at www.edt.training.